# WHY THEY SCRATCH THEMSELVES

## How to Understand Baseball

JOHN W. HOOD

Cover Illustration: Dave Allen
Text Illustrations: Richard McCoy

Forward Press
Tinley Park, Illinois

# Contents

The First

# Play Ball!

## Introduction

One day I was watching a baseball game on television. My longtime friend, Susan, sat reading on the couch. Occasionally, I would say things to the TV such as "Bad call", "Bleep"[1], and finally, "We need a sacrifice fly."

At this point Susan looked up from her book, "That sounds very cruel," she said.

Baseball does have some odd traditions, but pulling the wings off flies is not one of them.

Susan's comment highlights her view of the game as a peculiar male ritual. It is not. In fact, to the fan, baseball is closer to romance than sport.

◆ ◆ ◆ ◆

**There are only three types of events in a baseball game**!

I named them the Must Play, the May Play, and the Automatic Play. These events are easy to understand and explain everything that the players may or must do in a baseball game. You will be able to understand what is happening in a baseball game after reading Chapter Two.

But first, a little general information . . .

---

1. 'Bleep' is a term denoting an unprintable expletive.

John W. Hood

# The Field

Take a look at the last page of the book. It is a foldout illustration of a baseball field. Let's get out on the field.

Step into the batter's box. Now look into the outfield. To your left, the left fielder is nonchalantly scratching himself. Scanning to the right, the center fielder and the right fielder squint slightly as they await the pitch. The pitcher paws at the mound impatiently while you get ready.

Take a few loose and easy practice swings. The wood bat feels light and natural in your hands. Your feet scratch at the dirt, digging in, and you crouch in a comfortable batting stance. You tap home plate, then bring the bat back and up to a vertical position. Cocked and ready. You look out to the pitcher. He stands frozen, staring in at the catcher.

You stand perfectly still . . . holding your breath . . .

You watch the pitcher swing his arms in a rhythmic motion then stride forward. Suddenly, a shiny white flash hisses angrily before you. Muscles and nerves trigger in a controlled panic and your bat licks across home plate.

Thwack! The satisfying thump of wood against leather. The ball rises in a high arc over the shortstop's head. Blood pumping, you pound toward first base. You look over to see the ball drop in left field. Then you see the left fielder fumble the ball just as your right foot slams clumsily into the hard canvas bag – first base. Instantly, you turn for second base. Seeming to arrive in three long strides, you slide smoothly on a hip across the soft dirt into second base.

You look up at the umpire standing over the base. His arms fly out wide. "Safe!"

Dust yourself off. And wipe that bubble gum off your face. You just got a base hit.

Did you understand what happened here? If not, don't worry. You will.

Baseball is not a game that can be learned piecemeal from your Resident Baseball Expert's (or ResBex's) detailed explanation of a particular play. A ResBex could be your spouse, parent, child, friend, co-worker, or anyone who 'knows' baseball. In order to understand baseball, you need to know the basics or, in baseball lingo, the fundamentals.[2] They are easy to learn.

Baseball terms appear in bold the first time they are used. The glossary also defines all the highlighted terms.

## The Players: Pitchers, Batters, and Fielders

### Pitchers

The teams take turns playing offense and defense. The players standing on the field are the defensive team. A play starts when the pitcher **pitches** the ball to the catcher. The term 'pitch' may be a bit deceptive in that one associates pitching with hay or horseshoes while a baseball is thrown 80 to 90-plus miles per hour in professional baseball. The term was probably derived from the very genteel English game of cricket which may have been the inspiration for the game of baseball.[3]

### Batters

The player from the offensive team stands next to home plate holding a **bat**. The bat used in professional baseball is a tapered wooden club.

2. 'Fundamentals' is a baseball term referring to the proper execution of routine plays and basic skills.

3. In cricket, the ball is bounced off the ground or 'pitch'. Pitch is an English term for playing field.

In most other levels of baseball, the bat is made of aluminum.

The **batter** swings the bat while gripping the skinny end. He attempts to hit the ball with the fat end of the bat. Players on the offensive team take turns **batting**.

### Fielders

The defensive players, or **fielders**, wear padded leather **gloves** on one hand to catch a ball that has been hit by a batter or thrown by another fielder.[4] The glove is worn on the player's non-throwing hand. For example, a player who throws right-handed wears the glove on his left hand.

## The Object of the Game

Players on the offensive team attempt to advance to each base consecutively in a *counterclockwise* direction. Everyone has seen a young child hit the ball and excitedly run to third base – the wrong way. The batter tries to advance to first base, second base, third base, then

4. Many people refer to the glove as a **mitt**. They are somewhat different. A glove is divided into separate sections for the fingers, like work gloves. The catcher uses a mitt. With the mitt, the thumb fits in one section and the other fingers all fit in the other section, like an oven mitt. (The mitt does have separate sections inside for the fingers.) Both the glove and the mitt are hinged and connected by a leather webbing between the thumb and index finger. The mitt is more heavily padded. The catcher wears a mitt to protect his hand when catching pitches. The other fielders wear gloves. Incidentally, catching a ball does not hurt the hand. The ball is caught in the hinged area, between the thumb and index finger.

home plate. He may stop at a base and occupy that base while another player bats. A player scores a **run** if he touches home plate before his team makes three outs. The run is the only scoring unit in baseball.

The defensive team gets an **out** by preventing an offensive player from occupying a base. For example, if you hit the ball in the air and a fielder catches it, you are out. The ways to make an out are discussed in Chapter Two. The offensive player who is out must leave the playing field.

## The Batting Order

The teams take turns at batting or trying to score. Before the game each team's manager lists his players in the order in which they will bat. This is his team's **batting order**. He gives a copy to the other team's manager. The visiting team bats first. After the visitors have made three outs, the home team bats. After each team makes three outs, one **inning** is complete. There are nine innings in a Major League game.[5]

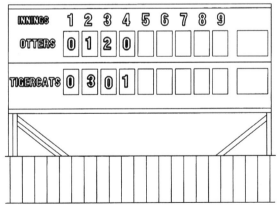

**Figure 1, The Scoreboard**
*The TigerCats lead 4-3 after four innings. It is the Otters' turn to bat in the fifth inning.*

5. There are seven innings in a softball game and most baseball games at or below the high school level.

# Types of Batted Balls

A batted ball that bounces along the ground is a **ground ball** or **grounder**. A ball hit in the air with some degree of arc is a **fly ball**. A fly ball that travels in a virtually straight line, or has very little arc, is called a **line drive**.

A high fly ball in the infield area, called a **pop fly** or **pop-up**, is the least desirable type of batted ball. The fielder has plenty of time to get under it and catch it for an out. On the other hand, a line drive is a ball hit very hard. Unless hit right at a fielder, a line drive won't be caught for an out.

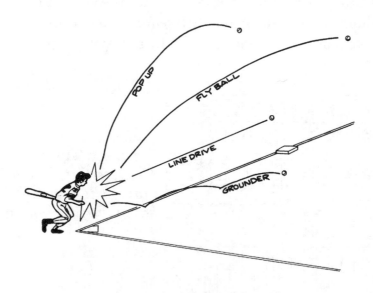

**Figure 2, Types of Batted Balls.**
*The paths of various types of batted balls.*

# Fair and Foul

Every ball batted is **fair** or **foul**. Whether a ball is fair or foul affects what a player may or must do, which is described in the next chapter.

White chalk powder is used to mark the **foul lines**. The area between the lines is **fair territory**. The **foul lines** themselves are also part of *fair* territory. **Foul territory** is the area outside the lines.

### Balls Hit in the Air

A fly ball caught in the air, or touched in the air when in fair territory, is a fair ball. A ball caught in the air or touched in the air when in foul territory is foul. You look to where the ball is located when touched or caught, not where the fielder's feet are located. Of course, when a fielder catches the ball in the air, the batter is out.

When a fly ball hits the ground without being touched you look to where the ball hit the ground — in front of or beyond first or third base (as the case may be). A fly ball landing beyond first or third base is fair if it lands in fair territory and foul if it lands in foul territory. Assume that you hit a looping fly ball over third base. The ball kicks up some chalk from the foul line. Fair ball!

What about balls that hit the ground before reaching first or third base?

**Ground Balls** (Including fly balls hitting the ground before reaching first or third base)**:**

### *If the ball is touched —*

A ball that hits the ground before it reaches first base or third base is fair if it is first touched when in fair territory and foul if first touched when in foul territory.

## *If the ball stops—*

If the ball stops without being touched before reaching first base or third base, as the case may be, the location of the ball when it stops determines whether it is foul or fair. For example, a weakly batted ball may begin rolling in fair territory then roll into foul territory and stop. Foul ball. If the ball rolled in foul territory then into fair territory, and stopped in fair territory without being touched, the ball is fair.

## If the ball travels beyond first or third base without being touched

The ball is fair if it passed over the base while it was in fair territory and foul if the ball was in foul territory at the instant that it passed the front edge of first or third base. You hit a ground ball that takes a high bounce in front of third base. The third base umpire, who stands behind third base, sights down the foul line. He calls the ball fair if it passes over third base (or to the infield side) and foul if it passes outside the base (in foul territory). These calls are usually the most controversial foul or fair calls that the umpire makes, sometimes resulting in arguments.

**Figure 3, Fair and Foul**
*Clearly, ground ball A is foul and ground ball B is fair. Ground ball C passed to the right of third base then bounced into foul territory. It is a fair ball because the ball was in fair territory at the moment that it passed the front edge of third base.*

Now — what happens in a baseball game?

The Second

# The Fundamentals

This chapter describes what the offensive players must or may do and how the player makes outs.

There are just three rules controlling whether a player is allowed to occupy a base or advance: the Must Play, the May Play, and the Automatic Play. The Must Play describes when the offensive players must try to advance. The May Play tells you when players may try to advance at their own risk. On the Automatic Play, certain players advance or are out automatically. [6]

The rules of baseball are easier to understand than, say, the rules of Monopoly or the rules of football or basketball, for that matter. The three 'plays' describe, with complete accuracy, ninety-nine per cent of events that occur in a baseball game! They are explained in just four short paragraphs and illustrated by liberal use of example. Subsequent chapters discuss strategy. You will not get lost.

First of all, a batter who occupies a base is called a **base runner** or **runner**. A base runner who occupies a base is said to be 'on' a base. For example, if a runner occupies first base there is "a runner on first". Only one runner is permitted to occupy any single base at one time. Therefore, there may be up to three runners occupying the three bases at once — a runner on first base, a runner on second base, and a runner on third base.

6. Caution: This is not baseball terminology. Don't use the terms or your ResBex (Resident Baseball Expert) will not understand what you are talking about.

# Must Plays

Batters and/or runners must do something on two types of batted balls: 1) the fair ball that hits the ground and, 2) a fair or foul fly ball caught in the air by a fielder.

## Fair Ball That Hits The Ground

**Fundamental: When the batter hits a fair ball that hits the ground the batter must attempt to advance at least as far as first base. The batter is absolutely entitled to occupy first base if he can make it safely. Since only one player may occupy a base at one time, a runner occupying first base must attempt to advance to second base safely. And, if first base is occupied when a fair ball hits the ground, then runners occupying *consecutive* bases after first base are also forced to advance.**

**Example:** Assume that there are runners on first base and second base. The batter hits a ground ball in fair territory. What must the offensive players do?

**Answer:** Fair ball hitting the ground!!! The batter must try to advance at least as far as first base. The batter is absolutely entitled to occupy first base if he can make it safely. The runner on first base is then 'forced' to advance to second base in order to avoid having two runners on one base. The runner on second base is, in turn, forced off his base by the runner who was on first base. The short answer is that the batter must attempt to advance to first base and the runners on first and second base must each attempt to advance one base or are **forced**.

**Example:** There are runners on first base and third base. The batter hits a ground ball in fair territory. What must the runners do?

10

**Answer:** Fair ball hitting the ground! The batter must try to advance to first base and the runner on first is forced to advance to second base.

So far so good. What about the base runner who was on third base?

The runner on third base is not forced to advance. Since there is no runner on second base there is no runner who would push him off his base. As will be explained later, the runner on third base may attempt to advance to home plate — to score a run — at his own risk. Or he may remain on third base. He is not 'forced' to do anything.

### When is a Runner Out or Safe?

On a play in which the runner and/or batter must try to advance one base the defensive player makes an out by holding the ball in his hand or glove and touching the base before the runner arrives, forcing him out.[7] The defensive player holding the ball will ordinarily **tag** the base with his foot. (But a fielder in possession of the ball can use his hand or glove or any part of his body to touch the base.) The batter or runner who is out must leave the playing field. On the same play, the runner is **safe** if he arrives before the fielder.

**Example:** There are no runners on base. The batter hits the ball on the ground. The shortstop catches the ball in his glove or **fields** the ball. What will the batter and the fielders do?

**Answer:** The batter must run to first. The shortstop will throw the ball to the first baseman. The first baseman, while holding the ball, must

---

7. On a fair ball hitting the ground, a batter is required to run to first. But, as a matter of baseball jargon, the batter is not said to be forced although this event is the same as the force play on the runner. Only runners already on base are said to be forced, not batters.

tag the base before the batter arrives to get him out. In practice, the first baseman will be standing with one foot on first base when he receives the throw. But, if the batter tags first base before the first baseman catches the ball, the batter is safe.

**Example:** There is a runner on first with no outs.[8] The batter hits a ground ball right at the second baseman. The second baseman fields the ball and decides to try to get an out at second base.

What happens on this play?

**Answer:** Offensively, the batter must run to first base. The runner on first is then forced to advance to second base. At the moment that the ball was hit, the shortstop starts running toward second base to receive a throw from the second baseman for the **force out**. Assume that the shortstop catches the second baseman's throw and tags second base before the runner arrives. The runner is out.

If the shortstop thinks he has time, he will throw to the first baseman to try to get the batter out, too. The first baseman will be standing with one foot on first base awaiting the shortstop's throw. If the shortstop's throw is caught by the first baseman (who tags first base) before the batter arrives, then the batter is out, too. That is a double out or a **double play**, so called because the defense gets two outs on one batted ball.[9]

8. In baseball lingo, when it is said that there is a 'runner on first' or 'man on first', it means that no other runners are on base. All the runners are accounted for in this way. For example, "There was a man on third, no outs . . .," means there was just a runner on third base and no other runners.

9. This type of double play occurs a couple of times each game on the average.

◆ ◆ ◆ ◆

When there is a runner on every base the **bases are loaded**.

**Example:** You are the pitcher. Bases loaded, no outs. The batter hits a ground ball that you field. What are you going to do with the ball?

**Answer:** When the bases are loaded there is a **force at every base**. You could throw to any base to get a force. Usually the pitcher tries for the force out at home plate, to prevent the runner from scoring. The catcher tags home plate and, if he has time, will throw to first base to get the batter out for a double play.[10]

A fair ball hitting the ground can also be a fly ball or line drive that nobody catches.

**Example:** You are the runner on first. The batter hits a fly ball that lands between the center fielder and the right fielder. What do you have to do?

**Answer:** Advance to second base. Obviously, you will make it easily. You can advance farther at your own risk. When a runner advances at his own risk, the fielder must physically tag him with the ball. This is discussed in May Plays.

Remember that when a fair batted ball hits the ground, the batter and a forced base runner must only advance <u>one</u> base. After safely advancing the one base, the batter and runner may attempt to advance farther at their own risk.

10. The batter must finish his swing before leaving home plate while the runners get a running start. Therefore, the catcher always has a better chance of getting the batter out than a runner.

# The Other Must Play: The Caught Fly Ball

The first type of Must Play discussed a fair ball that hit the ground. The second type of Must Play involves a fly ball, either fair or foul, that is caught.

**Fundamental: The batter is out when his fly ball, whether fair or foul, is caught in the air.** *After a fly ball is caught,* **a runner on base must tag the base that he occupied when the ball was hit. Often the runner will wait on the base until the catch is made. The runner is out if a defensive player holding the ball tags the base after the catch is made and before the runner returns to it. This is another type of double play because two outs are made on one batted ball.**

**Example:** There is a runner on second base. The batter hits a fly ball into right field. The runner does not think that the ball will be caught. He starts running while the ball is in the air, thinking he will be able to run all the way to home plate and score a run. Meanwhile, the right fielder makes a spectacular catch. He throws the ball to the shortstop who tags second base before the runner can return. The runner is out. Double play.

**Example:** There is a runner on first base. The batter hits a high pop fly that is caught by the shortstop. The runner, seeing that the ball would be caught, remained on first base. After making the catch, the shortstop sees the runner standing on first base. So the shortstop does not throw to his first baseman to attempt to get the runner out, since it would be useless. Instead, he simply returns the ball to the pitcher.

**Example:** There is a runner on first base. The batter hits a line drive to the right side of the infield. The runner thinks that the ball will get past the second baseman and fall in the outfield. He starts running to second base. The second baseman catches the ball and throws it to the first baseman who tags first base before the runner returns to it. The runner is out. Of course, the batter was out when the second baseman caught the ball. Another double play.

On the vast majority of fly balls, the runner will be able to anticipate when the ball will be caught and will return to safely tag his base. Most of the plays in which a runner is caught off his base are on caught line drives.

But, if the runner safely tags the base after a ball is caught, or **tags up**, then he can attempt to advance at his own risk.

The rest of the chapter is a piece of cake.

## May Plays

**The runner may try to advance at his own risk at any time that a Must Play is not in effect. The fielder must physically tag the runner with the ball (when the runner is not on a base) to get an out. A runner may try to advance at his own risk:**

- **when he is not forced and a fair ball hits the ground**

- **after he safely moves up one base on a force play or tags up after a caught fly ball**

- **when there is no batted ball. The ball is always in play except when an umpire calls time out.**

**Example:** Recall the example used earlier of runners on first and third base with no outs. The batter hits a fair ground ball. What must the runners do?

**Answer:** The runner on first, as we well know, is forced. The runner on third is not forced. The runner on third may try to score if he so chooses.

To get him out, the infielder must throw the ball to the catcher who tags the runner with the ball.

Assume that the runner on first was able to advance safely to second base. At the moment that he touched second base he could attempt to advance farther, if he so chose, at his own risk. The moment that the runner is safe at second base it becomes a May Play for him because, having advanced one base, he is not required to do anything else. Then, to get him out, the fielder has to physically tag him with the ball (when he is not on the base).[11]

**Example:** There is a runner on first. The pitcher's pitch is wild and bounces past the catcher. The runner may . . . ?

**Answer:** The runner may try to advance to second or farther if he dares. The defensive player must, of course, physically tag the runner to get him out. Notice that there is no batted ball on this play. May Plays do not necessarily require a batted ball. Must Plays always involve a batted ball.

**Example:** There is one out. You are on third base. It is the last half of the ninth inning. The batter hits a high fly ball into left field. You see that the left fielder will catch the ball. What are you going to do?

**Answer:** You may, if you dare, try to score after the catch.

You decide to try it. You wait in a crouched position, one foot on third base, looking back at the left fielder. At the moment that he catches

11. It is an allowable tag for a defensive player holding the ball in his glove to touch the runner with any part of the glove.

the ball you begin a frantic sprint for home.[12] You glimpse the catcher standing stoically over home plate as you and the ball converge on him. He reaches for the ball just as you slide across the plate. His glove whacks you on the shoulder. The umpire calls you . . . safe! You scored a run.

What happened here? The batter was out when the ball was caught. Two outs. You were allowed to leave your base at the moment that the ball was caught (touched, technically). It became a May Play. To get an out, the fielder had to tag you with the ball before you touched home plate.

This is a **sacrifice fly**. The batter is deemed to have sacrificed himself for the good of the team by intentionally hitting a fly ball and making an out in order to allow a teammate to score.[13]

Here is an example that challenges your grasp of the Must and May Plays. If you follow the fundamentals you will be able to figure it out easily. It is a common baseball play.

12. A runner can be called out if he leaves the base even a split second before the ball is touched (or catch is made). When the defensive team thinks that the runner on third, for example, **left the base early,** or **left early**, the pitcher must throw the ball to the third baseman after the play. The third baseman will tag the base. The umpire at third base will call the runner out if he left early. The act of requesting a ruling from an umpire is called an **appeal**. There is usually no appeal allowed at the high school baseball level and below. At these levels, the umpire simply calls the runner out if he left early.

13. Parenthetically — Can a runner try to advance after a foul fly that is caught? Yes.

**Example:** There is a runner on first with no outs. The batter hits a ground ball to the first baseman. He fields it just a step away from first base.

The runner, who is forced, runs to second base.

The first baseman elects to step on first base to get the batter out. Then he throws the ball to the shortstop to attempt to get the runner out at second base.

**Question:** Can the shortstop tag second base for a force out?

**Answer:** No.

At the moment that the first baseman tagged first base to get the batter out, the force play was no longer in effect. Remember that the reason that the runner was forced off his base was because the batter was required to run to first and absolutely entitled to occupy first base if he could have made it safely. The runner was forced off first when the ball was hit because two runners are not allowed on one base. Here, the first baseman got the batter out first by tagging first base. At the moment that the batter was out there was no possibility that two runners would occupy first base. The runner was no longer forced.

When the **force is off** it becomes a May Play for the runner (and fielders). The fielder has to physically tag the runner. The runner can even try to return to first if he so decides.

### Tagging a Runner Out

A runner can be tagged out whenever he is between bases. For instance, a fielder can tag a runner out on a Must Play instead of tagging the base. Assume that there is a runner on first base with no outs. The batter hits a ground ball to the second baseman. The runner is forced. The second baseman fields the ball and tags the runner before he reaches second base. The runner is out.

## When Does a Run Count?

There are runners on first and third base with one out. The batter hits a ground ball that is fielded by the shortstop. The fielders get the force out at second base on the runner and get the batter out at first base — a double play. There are three outs so the inning is over. But before the fielders complete the double play the runner on third base crosses home plate. Does that count as one run?

No. If the third out in the inning is gotten on a Must Play (a force out, getting the batter out at first base, or a caught fly ball), runners who cross the plate do not score a run. But if the third out is gotten on a May Play, and the runner scores before the out is made, then the run counts.

May Plays may be summarized simply. Any time that a Must Play is not in effect, a runner can try to advance at his own risk. To get him out, a fielder must physically tag the runner with the ball. Remember that a Must Play is no longer in effect at the moment that the runner is safe on a force play, or when he tags up after the catch, or when the force is off. When there is no batted ball it is always a May Play.

## The Automatic Play

The batter can also advance to first base automatically, without hitting the ball.

**Fundamental: The umpire standing behind home plate judges each pitch to be a 'ball' or 'strike'. A ball is an inaccurate pitch that does not pass through the 'strike zone'. If the pitcher throws four balls the batter is automatically awarded first base. This is called a 'base on balls' or a 'walk'. The batter is also automatically awarded first base if the pitch hits him.**

The batter is out after three strikes. This is called a **strike-out**.

## What is a Strike?

1. A strike is any pitch a batter swings at and misses entirely. Think of this as striking at the ball.[14]

2. A strike is a foul ball that is not caught in the air by a fielder.

Any caught fly ball is an out, whether caught in fair or foul territory. So, a foul ground ball is a strike and a foul fly no one catches is a strike. If a foul ball is not caught, the ball is returned to the pitcher. Runners are not allowed to advance.

3. A strike is an accurate pitch that the batter does not swing at which passes through the **strike zone**.

The strike zone may be thought of as a very delicate rectangular pane of glass extending upward from the front edge of home plate and levitating between the top of the batter's knees and the bottom of his breastbone. Any pitch that would break or barely chip the glass is a strike.[15]

14. One strikes at a snake. 'Strike', like pitch, is also one of those very civilized words that is, undoubtedly, derived from cricket.

15. Technically, the strike zone is a levitating box, not a levitating pane of glass. Project the entire surface of home plate upward. The bottom of the box is even with the top of the batter's knees. The top of the box is even with the midpoint between the batter's belt and shoulder. That five-sided box is the strike zone. But, for all practical purposes, the strike zone is a pane of glass. Want to have some fun? Ask a ResBex to define the strike zone. Most cannot identify it exactly.

The **home plate umpire calls** each pitch a ball or a strike.

**Figure 4,**

**The Strike Zone**

*The strike zone is shown as a pane of glass above the front edge of home plate. Any pitch that would break or even chip the imaginary pane of glass is a strike.*

## What is a Ball?

A **ball** is a pitch that the batter does not swing at which would not break the imaginary glass of the strike zone. Any pitch that a batter swings at is a strike, wherever that pitch is located.

After four balls the batter is awarded first base on a **base on balls**, also called a **walk**. After three strikes, the batter is out. There is one little exception. Three strikes and you're out, but — the batter is not out if the third strike is any foul ball that is not caught in the air. The batter is allowed an infinite number of such foul balls. But on the umpire's called third strike (a pitch that the batter does not swing at) or a swing and a miss, the batter is **out on strikes** or strikes-out.[16]

When the batter walks, then any base runner, or base runners, who would be 'forced' automatically move up one base.

### Describing the Location of Pitches

Players, fans, and commentators use the same lingo to describe the location of pitches. You simply indicate whether a pitch was inside or outside, high or low, relative to the strike zone. For example, assume that a right-handed batter is at bat. A pitch passes below the batter's knees and between the batter and home plate. The pitch is 'low and inside'. Suppose that a pitch passes over the outside edge of the plate but above the batter's breastbone. The pitch is said to be 'high'.

A pitch that passes over the edge of the plate farthest away from the batter and in the strike zone is 'over the outside corner'. The pitcher has 'hit the outside corner' for a strike. On the other hand, if such a pitch passes outside the strike zone for a ball, it is 'outside'. If the 'outside' pitch is also low, it is 'low and outside', or more commonly, 'low and away'. Suppose the pitcher throws a strike over the middle third of the plate. The pitch is 'down the middle' (of the plate).

## All You Need To Know

The Must Play, the May Play, and the Automatic Play are derived from how the fielders get outs. Here are the fundamentals again in short form. There <u>will</u> be a test (in the last chapter).

16. For ResBexes reading this book to look for errors, there is, of course, one other tiny exception which will be discussed later under 'bunting'. (Ha.)

## Must Plays

### *Fair Ball Hitting the Ground*

Offense: When a fair ball hits the ground the batter must try to reach first base. Runners occupying consecutive bases beginning with first base are forced to attempt to advance one base.

Defense: A fielder in possession of the ball need only tag the base before the runner arrives in order to make a force out.

### *Balls Caught in the Air*

Offense: After a caught fly ball, whether fair or foul, a runner must tag the base that he occupied.

Defense: The batter is out on a caught fly ball. After the catch, the fielder with the ball can also get the runner out by tagging the base before the runner returns to it.

## May Plays

Offense: When no Must Play is in effect the runner can try to advance at any time at his own risk. The Must Play is no longer in effect after the runner is safe on a force play or after he tags up after a caught fly ball.

Defense: The fielder must physically tag the runner (when the runner is not on a base).

## The Automatic Play

The batter is automatically awarded first base on four balls or when he is hit by a pitch.

Three strikes and you're out. Remember that a foul batted ball that is not caught does not count as the third strike. Unless it's a bunt.

That's all you have to know.

If you apply these rules and a little common sense, understanding the game will be a **can of corn**.[17]

# Confidence Builders

If you understand the **infield fly rule**, you understand baseball. It is the single esoteric rule in baseball. Another great thing about the infield fly rule is that chances are good that your ResBex probably does not understand it. The infield fly rule incorporates the May and Must plays. Do not be concerned if you cannot give the answer. You understand baseball if you simply understand the answer.

**Example:** There are runners on first and second base and no outs. The batter hits a pop-up. It will be an easy catch for the shortstop in the infield area.

While the ball is still in the air the umpire signals that the batter is out.

The umpire is enforcing the infield fly rule.

**Question:** Why was this rule put into the rule book?

**Hints:** Put yourself in a base runner's shoes. Consider what slightly dishonest play the infielders could make to turn this play into an easy double play.

**Answer:** The runner must tag up after a fly is caught. So the runners will stand on their bases waiting for the ball to be caught (Must Play). Then, if the shortstop catches the ball, the batter is out. The runners will certainly not try to tag up and advance after the catch (May Play). It would be an easy play for the shortstop to throw to second or third base, as the case might be, to get the runner out.

17. A high fly ball that is easy to catch.

Assume that the shortstop pretended he was going to catch the ball and instead, unscrupulously (this is baseball and not cricket after all), allowed the ball to drop to the ground. Fair ball hitting the ground!!! It then becomes a force play (Must Play). Then both runners must try to advance one base. The runners are standing on their respective bases (because it appeared to be a fly ball that would be caught). The runners don't have the benefit of the head start that they get on a ground ball or on a fair fly ball or line drive that will clearly not be caught.

The ball would fall in the infield, a short distance from the bases and, consequently, a short throw for the shortstop. The fielders could get an easy double play! The shortstop would throw to the third baseman who would step on third base then relay the ball to the second baseman, who would step on second.

The infield fly rule prevents this unfair result — an easy double play. The infield fly rule states that when runners are on first and second base (or the bases are loaded) with less than two outs and the batter hits a catchable fly ball in the infield area , the batter is out. The infield fly rule treats this situation just as though the fielder had caught the ball, regardless of whether he catches the ball or not. The umpire calls the batter out while the ball is still in the air.

The infield fly rule is the singular 'odd' rule in baseball. Now you understand the reason for the rule.

◆ ◆ ◆ ◆

Baseball is a simple game, not a peculiar male ritual. But if it was, you could now be said to be privy to the single secret of the inner circle of ResBexes — the infield fly rule — except for the fact that many ResBexes do not quite understand the rule.

There is one other little mystery. Why are the players always scratching themselves?

Players scratch themselves — actually pull on the crotch area of their uniforms — to adjust an item of personal equipment called a jock, or athletic supporter, which is worn in lieu of underwear.

Jocks have an elastic waistband with a triangular pouch in front and straps that fit around the buttocks. Jocks are designed to hold the player's . . . uh . . . vital organs in a stable position while running. It's a bra of sorts. Players occasionally need to reposition their . . . personal equipment.

Congratulations! Now that you know the fundamentals, you understand the rules. That's all there is to it. We now go into the fun part — strategy. Fundamentals will also be reviewed in the context of the strategy discussions. You will not get lost.

# The Batter And The Pitcher

The pitcher/batter confrontation is the elemental component of a baseball game. *All* baseball strategy decisions are ultimately based on the match-up between pitcher and batter. This chapter explains what the pitcher and batter are trying to do.

## Batting

### Right-handed and Left-handed Batters

A right-handed batter uses the batters box on the third base side of home plate. He grips the bat with his right hand above his left hand. A left-handed batter stands in the box on the first base side of the plate. His top hand on the bat is his left hand. Some players, called **switch-hitters,** are able to bat both left and right-handed.

### Pulling the Ball

When a right-handed young man develops some strength he discovers that he hits the ball hardest when the bat is in the following zone.

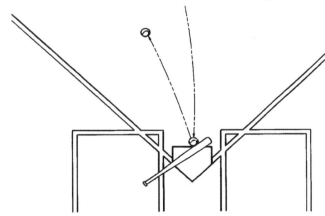

**Figure 5, Pulling the Ball**
*This illustration shows the position of the bat of a right-handed batter when he 'pulls the ball'.*

Of course, the ball that he hits travels to the left. This is called **pulling the ball**. A large majority of the time a right-handed batter will time his swing to pull the ball or hit it to the left side of the field. Left-handed batters pull the ball to the right side of the field.

### The Timing of the Swing

Hitting a pitch at any level of baseball is difficult. It looks easy. The batter just takes a good, hard swing at a ball, right?

A batting swing is a lot like a golf swing — except that the ball is moving. The swing requires coordinating a shift of weight while moving the arms in an arc. Before the pitch, the batter stands poised in a slight crouch holding the bat vertically. The batter's weight is on the leg farther away from the pitcher or **back leg**. As the pitch is thrown the batter strides forward about half a step with the front foot, transferring his weight to both feet. His body turns and his hands come forward as he begins to swing the bat. He takes a level swing at the ball.[18]

The batter (at any level of baseball) has much less than one second to decide whether to swing at a pitch. In the Major Leagues, a thrown ball takes less than one-half second to get to home plate. The batter has a fraction of that half-second to decide whether to start his swing. Once he starts his swing it's impossible to correct it.

A batter hits a ball hardest when he pulls it because the bat has the most speed when it is in the 'pull zone'. If the batter triggers his swing too late, he may miss the ball. If he does **swing late,** yet makes contact with the ball, he will hit it to the other side of the field or **opposite field**. The opposite field is the side of the field opposite the side to which the batter naturally pulls the ball.

18. This is a simplistic explanation of hitting. Numerous books have been written on the subject of batting alone.

## The Sweet Spot

A certain area of the bat is much more lively or springy than other places: the **sweet spot**.

The ball will spring off the bat when hit here. Hitting a ball on the sweet spot accounts for the exciting 'crack of the bat' heard when a batter hits the ball well. The crack of the bat is actually a loud sharp click. Balls hit on other parts of the bat have much less force or power and make a heavier sound, more like a 'clunk'. Anyone who has played pinball knows that the ball springs off a particular area of the lever. There is a live spot about two-thirds of the way down the lever that is analogous to the sweet spot on a bat. Steel balls hit off the area nearest the hinge or the far end of the lever do not travel as well. Because a batter naturally pulls the ball, it's much easier for him to hit the ball on the sweet spot if the pitch travels over the middle or inside part of the plate.

So what is the batter's Achilles heel?

The outside corner.

## The Outside Corner

The batter must time his swing almost perfectly to hit a pitch over the outside of the plate. It will be difficult to hit the pitch with **power** (hit it far) because the pitch is outside of the batter's power zone. In contrast, even a batter who mistimes his swing may hit a pitch over the center or inside of the plate because the bat will be in that zone for a longer period of time during his swing. The key to hitting the outside pitch, and batting in general, is triggering the swing at exactly the right moment in order to hit the ball on the sweet spot. To do so requires instant recognition of the speed and location of the pitch.

A pitcher will attempt to **hit the outside corner** with his pitches.

In addition, the pitcher is rarely generous enough to throw the ball straight.

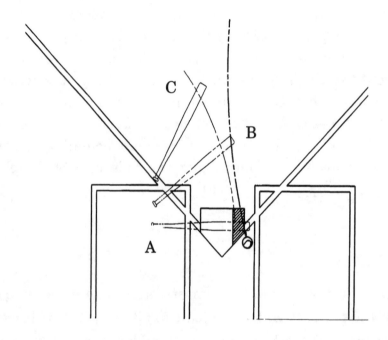

**Figure 6, The Outside Corner**

*The outside corner is shaded. This illustration shows the path of the bat during a right-handed batter's swing. The batter started his swing too soon and missed the pitch. Positions A and B show the start of the swing. Position C shows the position of the bat when the ball passed it.*

**What Happens to the Pitches that the Batter Hits.**

There is an old saying in baseball that "the ball is round and the bat is round and the batter is supposed to hit the ball square (sic)"[19]

The batter takes a level swing. So the closer to the center of the ball that the bat strikes, the better the chance the batter has to hit a hard line drive.

A line drive is the most desirable batted ball because the fielders have less time to react to the ball. Unless it is hit right at a fielder the ball will usually fall safely in the outfield. On the other hand, infielders have plenty of time to run under and catch a pop-up, which is the least desirable type of hit.

# Pitching

### Types of Pitches

Most pitchers at or above the high school level have at least three types of pitches. Most commonly, a pitcher throws (1) a **fastball**, (2) either a **curve** or a **slider** (they are different) and, (3) a **change-up** (short for change in speeds) — a slowball. Some pitchers throw other types of pitches, but these are by far the most common.

### — *The Fastball*

A fastball is just that. A very good Major League fastball is thrown at 90-plus M.P.H. An excellent fastball seems to jump up about an inch, or 'hop' just as it reaches home plate. It doesn't — it's an optical illusion.

However, a good fastball is not a straight pitch. A pitcher throws the fastball so that it moves slightly to the pitcher's right or left just as it reaches home plate. It drops slightly, too. A good fastball has **movement**, making it more difficult to 'hit square(ly).'

19. Like most baseball sayings, it's not grammatically correct.

## — *The Curveball*

The curveball, when thrown by a right-handed pitcher, moves from his right to his left. The pitcher grips the ball across the seams and snaps his wrist sharply downward in order to impart spin to the ball. The pitch moves a couple inches to the side just before it reaches home plate. A good curveball also drops dramatically. This is not an optical illusion. A curveball travels more slowly than a fastball.

## — *The Slider*

A slider is a hybrid of the fastball and the curveball. It travels almost as fast as a fastball and it curves and drops a little less than a curveball. When it came into vogue in the mid-1960's, batters disdainfully called the slider a 'nickel curve' because it only curves slightly. Apparently they did so to discourage pitchers from throwing it. A slider is sort of a trick fastball. It looks like a fastball until just before it reaches the plate, when it suddenly drops and curves. A good slider is very hard to hit.

Sliders and curveballs are called **breaking balls** because they change directions suddenly, breaking sideways and down.

## — *The Change-Up*

The change-up is a slowball. The pitcher uses the change-up when he thinks the batter expects a fastball or slider. The change of speed of the pitch throws the batter's timing off.

A good pitcher uses exactly the same throwing motion for all of his pitches. How can he throw a slow pitch with same arm motion as, say, a fastball? To throw a change-up, the pitcher holds the ball in his palm or between his fingers instead of firmly gripping the ball with his fingers like other pitches. The pitcher can use the same arm speed as a fastball but the ball travels much more slowly.

## Pitcher-Catcher Signals

Who decides which pitch to throw?

The pitcher is the boss. The pitcher and catcher communicate by signals. Because of the different speeds and movements of the pitches the catcher must know what pitch the pitcher will be throwing so he can prepare to catch it.

A number is assigned to each pitch. Usually, the fastball is number one, the curve or slider (whichever pitch the pitcher throws) is number two, and the change-up is number three. When the catcher squats in his position behind home plate, he signals a pitch by holding down one, two, or three fingers between his legs. The batter, who is looking at the pitcher, does not see the signs. If the pitcher does not want to throw the pitch that the catcher signals, he will shake his head or glove slightly. This is known as **shaking off the sign**. The catcher then puts down the sign for a different pitch. Some pitchers will affirm with a nod when a catcher signals the pitch that the pitcher wants to throw. Others just shake off signs for pitches they don't want to throw.

## Accuracy of the Pitches

It is one thing to throw a strike and another thing to throw a **good strike**. What a ResBex would call a good strike, or an effective pitch, depends on the game situation and pitcher's strategy. But, generally, certain pitches should be thrown in certain locations.

The strike zone was described as a levitating pane of glass. Visualize a window about one-half the size of the strike zone centered in the middle of the strike zone. A pitcher never wants to throw any pitch through the middle window or 'down the middle'. That's the batter's power zone; generally speaking, a good fastball or slider is effective when thrown anywhere else in the strike zone.

A good curveball or change-up, however, is thrown knee-high over the outside part of the plate away from the batter's power zone. That is, there is a much smaller target for a curve or change-up than a fastball or slider. Considering the dramatic movement of the curveball and fine touch required for the change-up, these are generally more difficult pitches to throw accurately. They are also the more difficult pitches to hit. A pitcher able to consistently throw good strikes, or throw his pitches where he wants them, is said to have good **control**.

## Righty v. Lefty and Righty v. Righty

A right-handed pitcher has more of an advantage over a right-handed batter than a left-handed batter. And the left-handed pitcher has more of an advantage over a left-handed batter than a right-handed batter. It is easiest to remember that the 'same-handedness advantage' goes to the pitcher.

Why?

The batter's power zone, or 'pull zone', is the middle and inside part of home plate. A right-handed pitcher's curves or sliders move *away from* the right-handed batter's power zone toward the outside of the plate. Even if these pitches are not quite as accurate as the pitcher would like, they move away from the power zone.

Also, the right-handed batter cannot immediately distinguish a fastball from a curveball or a slider thrown by a right-handed pitcher. All of the pitcher's pitches look alike when he releases them. If the batter is right-handed and the pitcher is right-handed then the batter may think, in the split second that he has to decide whether to swing, that the pitch is a fastball over the middle of the plate. If it is a curve or a slider which ends up on the outside of the plate the batter is left lunging helplessly, having started his swing too early.

On the other hand, a right-handed pitcher's curves and sliders will move *toward* the left-handed batter's power zone. For a right-handed pitcher to hit the outside corner on a left-handed batter, the pitcher has to start his curveball or slider outside the plate and try to nip the outside corner. First, the batter immediately identifies it as a breaking pitch. Secondly, if the pitcher does not start the pitch far enough outside, it will break over the middle or inside of the plate. Therefore, a right-handed pitcher is much more limited in pitches that he can successfully throw to a left-handed batter. He will throw mainly fastballs. He can throw any pitch to a righty.

As will be seen, the 'handedness' of the pitcher and batter is a <u>major</u> factor in strategy decisions.

**The Count**

How does a pitcher decide which type of pitch to throw at any particular time?

Suppose the batter **takes** two pitches, or lets them go by without swinging. The umpire calls the pitches 'balls'. The batter grounds the third pitch foul for a strike. The **count** is now two balls and one strike, or 'two and one'. Balls are counted first, then strikes. The count is the most important factor in the pitcher's decision as to what pitch to throw next.

The pitcher and batter each tries to get the count in his favor. When there are more balls than strikes, the count is in the batter's favor. When there are more strikes than balls, it's in the pitcher's favor. A 3-0 count (three balls and no strikes) or a 3-1 count is very favorable to the batter because the pitcher must throw a strike. If he throws a ball, the batter walks (advances to first base automatically). What pitch will the pitcher throw on these counts? A fastball. A fastball is the easiest pitch to control and has the largest target area. But it is also the easiest pitch to hit, especially when the batter knows that the fastball is coming.

On the other hand, an 0-2 or 1-2 count is favorable to the pitcher. The batter cannot afford to take a strike since he would strike out. On an 0-2 count the pitcher will usually try to induce the batter to swing at a bad pitch out of the strike zone. Even if the pitch is a ball, the count goes to 1-2 which is still to the pitcher's advantage. The batter cannot anticipate a particular pitch. He must swing at any pitch that may be called a strike. The pitcher can throw whatever pitch he wants to.

## What are the Pitcher and Batter Trying to Do?

The pitcher-batter duel is the basic element of a baseball game. First, the pitcher will be aware of strategies that the offensive team may be using. A certain type of pitch or location of a pitch may help defeat a certain offensive strategy. Secondly, a pitcher will have one pitch that he throws the best. For example, he may throw a very good fastball or an excellent curveball. At the Major League level, the pitcher also knows the type of pitches that the batter hits the best. Most Major League batters are good fastball hitters but some hit the low pitches better and some hit the high pitches better. Many have trouble with a good curveball.[20] The batter knows what pitch the pitcher throws best. The batter/pitcher confrontation becomes a cat-and-mouse game.

As a general rule, a pitcher will try to stay ahead on the count, work on the outside corner of the plate, and change the speeds of his pitches. He will not throw all fastballs even if that is his best pitch. If he did the batter would be able to time his swing.

20. A very common lament among former baseball players who failed to advance to the next level is, "I couldn't hit the curveball."

## Changing Speeds

Good control, or the ability to throw good strikes in the desired location, is the most important skill for a pitcher. However, the pitcher must change speeds effectively. Changing speeds simply means not throwing the same pitch too often. This keeps the batter from timing the pitch. The pitcher throws a variety of pitches such as the fastball, curve, and change-up. Each of the pitches travels at a different speed with different movement.

An explanation of the use of the change-up provides a dramatic illustration of what the pitcher is trying to do. Hitting a pitch well requires nearly perfect timing.

The pitcher will throw a change-up when the batter is not expecting it in order to catch him literally off balance. You are the pitcher. You have an excellent fastball. On the first pitch, you throw the fastball which the batter swings at and misses for a strike. The count is 0-1. Then you throw a curveball which is outside and is called a ball. The count is 1-1. The batter figures that you will try to get the count in your favor. He expects a fastball, your strongest pitch. You throw a change-up. The batter rocks forward. The magic moment when he anticipated the fastball arrives and passes. He stands flatfooted, his forward momentum spent, as old Mr. Slowball finally arrives. The batter is fooled and has no chance to hit the ball well.

On the other hand, a badly concealed, expected, or too slowly thrown change-up is usually hit hard.

Conversely, a pitcher with a very good fastball will often be able to throw the ball by or past the batter. A batter who is not expecting a fastball will not be able to trigger his swing in time. By the time that he gets his bat around, the ball is past him. A pitcher who has an excellent fastball will often throw it over the *inside* of the plate. This gives the batter less time to get his bat around far enough to pull the ball on the sweet spot.

**The Brushback Pitch**

Another method used to keep the batter off balance is to intentionally throw a fastball an inch or two from his ribs. Such a pitch is called a **brushback pitch**. Like the change-up, the pitch works against the batter's momentum. The batter begins to bring his momentum forward as the pitcher releases the pitch. Suddenly, a 90 mile-an-hour fastball is screaming at him. The intent of the pitch is to instill in the batter the raw fear of being hit by a pitch. Effectively thrown, the brushback pitch will cause the batter to either stumble ungracefully backwards or to tilt forward on the balls of his feet with his arms out as the ball passes by his chest. Naked fear grips him for a moment. After the pitch, his instinctive reactions become tentative and conscious. Because of primitive self-preservation instincts (no doubt dating back to the beginning of time), the batter's natural reactions become mechanical. He is more likely to hang back a little on the next pitch. For this reason, the brushback pitch is almost always followed by a curve or a slider on the outside part of the plate.

Of course, occasionally the brushback pitch does hit the batter.

The Fourth

# Baseball Skills and Lingo

This chapter fills in the practical aspects of a baseball game such as how far a batter will be able to advance on a batted ball and skills that the different fielders must possess. It also introduces some simple shorthand language before discussing offensive and defensive strategies.

## Time and Distance

You need only watch a game or two to get a sense of whether a batter or runner will be safe or out when trying to advance on a particular batted ball. These examples give you a very rough scale. Various factors are involved in a play, such as how hard and where the ball was hit, how fast the runner is, and how strong the fielder's throwing arm is. The rough estimates are mine.

1. On a fair ball that hits the ground, an outfielder will never be able to throw out the batter at first base or get a force on a runner. The ball takes too long to get to the outfielder and he has a long throw. During this time the batter (and any runner) will be able to advance at least one base easily.

2. The large majority of the time, a runner on first will make it to third base on a fair line drive hitting the ground in right field. Notice how far the throw is from right field to third base.

On a line drive hitting the ground in center field, a runner on first base will make it to third base less than half the time, and on a liner to left, only about 15% of the time. Notice that the left fielder has a short throw to third base. The major factor in whether a runner will be able to advance to third base is exactly where in the outfield the ball is hit.

*Importantly, a runner on second will usually score on any ball hitting the ground in the outfield.* Again, the reason is the time it takes for the ball to get to the fielder and the distance of the throw — from the outfield to home plate.

3. A shortstop will be successful in throwing out the batter (or runner on a force play) on about 90% of the balls that he gets to. But a shortstop, at any level of baseball, usually will not be able to fumble a ground ball and still throw out the batter at first base. Even on an ordinary ground ball that he **fields cleanly**, the shortstop usually throws out the batter by only two or three steps.

## Skills of the Fielders

Nine players play for each team at any one time. Each defensive position requires a slightly different skill.

### The Outfielders

Outfielders have to cover a lot of ground and throw a long distance. Therefore, good speed and a strong throwing arm are assets sought in outfielders. The center fielder has to cover the most ground so he is usually the fastest outfielder and often he is the fastest player on the team. The right fielder has the longest throw to make to a base — the throw to third base — so he almost always has the strongest throwing arm among the outfielders. To play left field, a very strong arm or great speed is not required. Of course, if he has one or both it is an asset.

### The Infielders

Infielders must react to the ball faster because they are closer to the batter. Most batters are right-handed and pull the ball, so the third baseman and shortstop have the most balls hit to them. The third baseman, shortstop, and second baseman must throw right-handed because otherwise the fielder would have to make a **pivot** to throw to first base.

Make a pivot?

The throw to first base to throw out a batter on a ground ball is the most common throw that the fielders have to make. Assume that a ground ball is hit directly at a right-handed second baseman. He is in his natural throwing position when he fields the ball. The second baseman simply anchors and pushes off his right foot and steps toward the first baseman with his left foot to throw the ball. A left-handed second baseman, on the other hand (pun intended), leads with his right foot when throwing. So, after fielding the ball he would have to make a $180^0$ turn (turn his back to home plate) and stride, before throwing. That is a pivot. Critical time is lost. That is why there are no left-handed second basemen in most 13-year-old and older leagues. And no left-handed shortstops or third basemen. For other positions, left-handedness is not a disadvantage.[21]

However, making certain pivots during a game is unavoidable. A fielder must make a pivot on any play in which the fielder's feet are not in throwing position when he fields or catches a ball. Assume that a runner is on first. The batter hits a ground ball to the shortstop. The

21. Your ResBex will tell you (smugly, perhaps) that there are no left-handed catchers in Major League baseball, either. The left-handed catcher must pivot to throw to third base. This is an important throw. Major League baseball is played at such a high level of skill that left-handedness is considered a disadvantage for a catcher. At nonprofessional levels of baseball, a left-hander can be a catcher.

shortstop decides to go for the double play. He throws to the (right-handed) second baseman. The second baseman tags second base and now must pivot. He must pivot because he catches the ball facing the shortstop with his momentum going forward. He must then turn to throw to first base. The second baseman's pivot on the attempted double play is the most common pivot.

Importantly, a base runner will have a better chance to advance on any play in which the fielder's feet are not in throwing position. Assume that a runner is on second base with no outs. The batter hits a fly ball between the center fielder and the right fielder. The right-handed center fielder catches it on the run. His momentum is going toward right field. The runner would have a good chance to advance to third base after tagging up after the catch. In order to throw to third base, the center fielder must stop, then make a $180^0$ turn in order to plant his right foot. Stopping and pivoting consume valuable time.

Let's go around the infield. The third baseman's position is usually called the **hot corner** because he is so close to the batter and many hard hit balls are pulled at him. He needs excellent reflexes and a strong throwing arm since he has a long throw to first base.

The best fielder on the team is the shortstop. Most batters are right-handed and naturally pull the ball to his position. So the shortstop has the most ground balls hit to him. The shortstop has a lot of territory to cover and a long throw to first base. He must be a cat-quick and smooth fielder. Ordinarily, he will not throw out the batter at first base if he fumbles a ground ball. He must have a strong arm.

The second baseman has a shorter throw to first base. He does have a difficult throw to make when pivoting on an attempted double play. The second baseman has fewer balls hit to him than the shortstop. He can usually throw a runner out at first base even if he fumbles a ground ball. Therefore, playing the position does not require quite the same fielding skill as the shortstop position.

Playing the first base position requires the least skill of the infield positions. The first baseman does not have as many balls hit to him as the other infielders. He docs not have to make too many throws. The first baseman handles the ball more than the other infielders because he receives throws on almost every out at first. But he does not need the same agility and fielding skills of the other infielders.

The catcher must have a very strong throwing arm. He must be able to make a strong throw to all the bases. He must be quick and skillful enough to catch or block wild pitches. Speed is not a requirement. In fact, catchers are notoriously slow.

Players who are good hitters but who do not have good fielding skills are commonly 'hidden' at first base or in left field.

A player may be able to play more than one position. Such a player is referred to as a **utility** player or **utility man**. Having a utility man on the roster gives a manager flexibility during a game in making substitutions.

Pitchers have to field ground balls and have some other fielding duties. A Major League pitcher will not play any other position. Pitching is a specialty so pitchers just pitch.[22]

22. These descriptions apply to play at the level of high school and above. In the lower leagues, the best players usually pitch, or play shortstop. The younger or less skilled players are put at second base and in right field. I played a lot of right field. It's very peaceful out there.

# Names for Hits

In general, the batter is credited with a **base hit** if he is successful in safely reaching any base on a batted ball — without causing a runner to make an out and without the benefit of a fielder's mistake or error.

A batter who, on his batted ball, safely advances to first base is credited with a **single**. If the batter makes it to second base safely on a ball that he hits, that's a **double**. Making it to third on his batted ball is a **triple**. And a ball that the batter hits over the outfield fence in fair territory is a **home run**. On a home run, the batter ceremoniously trots around the bases, touching each one in order.[23]

But the batter is <u>not</u> credited with a hit if the fielders could have gotten the batter out, but tried to get a runner out instead. For example, the batter is not credited with a hit if the fielders get a force out on a runner on the ball that the batter hit. The net effect of the force out is that one out was made on the batted ball and the batter takes a runner's place on first base. The batter has caused an out. The batter is not credited with a single when the fielder almost certainly could have gotten the batter out, but attempts, *successfully or unsuccessfully*, to get a runner out instead. In both cases the batter reaches base on a **fielder's choice**.

The batter is <u>not</u> credited with a hit if the fielders make an **error**. An error is any play in which fielders should have gotten an out on the batter or forced runner, but flubbed the play. Assume that the batter hits a ground ball right at the shortstop. The shortstop knocks the ball down but does not field it cleanly. By the time the shortstop picks the

23. There is such a thing as an **inside-the-park home run**. This is a rare, freak play in which the outfielder falls down or the ball takes a crazy bounce off the outfield wall and the batter is able to circle the bases to score.

ball up and throws to first base, the batter is safe. The batter would have been out if the shortstop had fielded the ball cleanly. The batter is not given a single. Instead, the shortstop is given an error. A fielder is given an error for any play which he should have gotten an out (or should have prevented a runner from advancing and failed to do so). More generally, an error is assigned on any play that a fielder clearly flubs or goofs up.[24]

Generically, singles, doubles, triples and home runs are called **hits.** The terms for hits are used as shorthand to describe an event. Instead of saying "Bob Reynolds hit a fair ball that hit the ground and he was able to advance as far as first base safely without causing any outs to be made, without the occurrence of a fielder's choice, and without an error having been made," one can say, "Bob Reynolds singled." As a practical matter, any runner on base will be able to advance at least as many bases as the batter. The runners will often be able to advance one more base than the batter on balls hit into the outfield.

The ratio of hits to bats is used to measure a batter's batting ability. The number is always expressed as a three digit number. In other words, if a batter gets 100 hits in 400 at-bats his **batting average** is 100 divided by 400, or .250. Batting averages give an estimate of a player's ability.

Also, a player's individual batting statistics tell you whether he hits with good power. A **power hitter** is one who hits a relatively high number of home runs and doubles. A triple is an unusual hit. In the Major Leagues, for example, a batter who hits 20 or more home runs

24. Another technical note for the benefit of picky ResBexes: Assume that a batter advances safely to second base without the benefit of an error or a fielder's choice. On the same play, the batter tries for third base and is thrown out. The batter is credited with a double even though he is out and will not occupy a base after the play.

is a power hitter. On the other hand, there are a number of players who seldom hit home runs, almost all their hits are singles. But that player may have a high batting average, meaning that he gets base hits a high percentage of the time. The single is by far the most common hit in baseball. As a rough gauge, about 70% of a player's total hits will be singles. Even the best Major League home run hitters hit a home run only once in every fifteen to twenty at bats.

Errors and hits are just statistics. The manager takes statistics into account in strategy considerations but the only thing that counts in a game is how many runs each team scores. The objective observer who judges plays to be hits or errors is called the **official scorer**.

## Describing Hits and Outs

Like hits, types of outs can be described in short form. For example, when a batter hits a line drive that is caught by the shortstop for an out, the batter is said to have 'lined out to the shortstop' or 'lined out to short'. Assume that a batter hits a ground ball that is fielded by the third baseman, who throws the batter out at first base. The batter has 'grounded out to third'. 'Third' refers to the third baseman. Similarly, a batter who 'flied out to left' hit a fly ball that was caught by the left fielder.

Parts of the field are also used to describe the location of the ball for both hits and outs. 'Shallow' and 'deep' denote outfield depths. The one-third or so of the outfield area nearest the infield is called **shallow** left, center, or right field. The outfield area ten to fifteen feet from the fence or wall is called **deep** left, center, or right field. A ball that is hit **down the line** is a ball that travels near the right or left field foul line. **Left-center** is the area of the field between left field and center field.

**Right-center**, of course, is the area between right field and center field. The **gap**, however, is the area between the left fielder and the center fielder or the center fielder and the right fielder. That is, left-center is a spot on the field while the 'gap' in left-center is the area between where the left fielder and center fielder are actually positioned.

A batter may 'fly out to deep right field', meaning that he has hit a fly ball that was caught by the right-fielder near the right field fence. The batter is said to 'double into the gap in left-center' if his batted ball travels between the left fielder and center fielder and the batter is able to advance safely to second base.

In the infield area, the area over second base is called **the middle**. A batter who hits a ground ball over second base is said to hit the ball 'up the middle' or 'through the middle'. The area between the third baseman and the shortstop is called **the hole**. For example, a shortstop fields a ball 'in the hole'.

Finally, baseball language describes the positioning of the fielders. For example, assume a right-handed batter is at bat. If the fielders expect the batter to pull the ball, they will take a few steps to the batter's left. The fielders are **playing the batter to pull**. If the fielders do not expect a batter to pull, they may play **straightaway**. The center fielder is positioned in line with home plate and second base, and the left fielder and right fielder are the same distance away from the left field foul line and right field foul line, respectively.

## The Roster and the Batting Order

A team has twenty-five players on its roster. The number may vary depending on the level of baseball, but twenty-five is pretty standard. Usually a Major League team will have ten or eleven pitchers. The rest of the players are infielders and outfielders. A nonpitcher is called a

**position** player. An infielder or an outfielder may be able to play more than one position but a player is most often used at one particular position. For instance, a shortstop may be able to play second base and/or third base, too, since the positions require similar skills. In Major League baseball, pitchers do not play any other position.[25]

The manager selects his players for a game and writes their names on a card in a batting order. Immediately before the game begins each

**Figure 7, The Batting Order**
*The line-up cards show the order in which the players will bat, or the team's 'batting order' and the positions that they will play.*

25. Pitchers are allowed to play other positions but it is not done in Major League baseball because there is always a position player on the bench with more experience as a fielder.

manager gives a copy of his batting order to the other manager and to the home plate umpire.

The batters will take turns batting in this order. In the first inning, Ford will bat first, then Sanchez, etc. If Charles makes the last out in the first inning (the third out), for example, Dodds then will bat first, or **lead off**, in the second inning, etc. The manager cannot change the order after he hands it to the umpire. The manager can, however, substitute other players for players in the original batting order during the game. The substitute takes the place of the player he replaces in the batting order. The replaced player leaves the game and cannot return.[26]

Usually, the first two batters are fast runners who are good at **getting on base,** but don't hit with much power. The first two batters will try to get on base by a walk or a hit, usually a single. The third and fourth batters are the team's best overall hitters. They hit more doubles and home runs. (A triple is an infrequent hit.) Their role is to **drive the runner(s) in**. The player filling the fourth position in the batting order is called the **cleanup hitter** because his job is to clear the runners off the bases (score them) with a long hit. The fifth through eighth positions in the batting order are generally filled in accordance with the player's overall hitting ability with the better hitters batting first. In Major League baseball, the pitcher always bats ninth. The pitcher

26. At some nonprofessional levels of baseball, the rules allow a player to reenter a game. The rationale for such a rule is to allow more players to play. A manager can put his substitutes in the game when his team is several runs ahead, then reinsert his starting players if his team loses some of the lead.

is not required to bat last, but Major League pitchers are almost invariably poor hitters.[27]

While a batter is at the plate, the next batter due to bat stands in the **on deck circle** to await his turn.

Now we have filled in the big picture. You will be able to better visualize the plays that are described in the next chapter.

27. O.K., O.K., ResBexes. There are two Leagues in Major League Baseball — the American League and the National League. The American League uses the **designated hitter**. The designated hitter bats for the pitcher (i.e., the pitcher does not bat). The obvious reason for the **DH** rule is that pitchers are poor hitters. Some other levels of baseball allow a designated hitter to bat in place of any player that the manager chooses (not just the pitcher).

# Offensive Strategy

Now, the team at bat is going to try to score.

## Scoring Position

Much offensive strategy involves trying to get a runner into **scoring position**. Scoring position is baseball slang for a runner on second or third. From second base a runner usually scores on any safe hit to the outfield, even a single. This is because of time and distance factors — the time that it takes for the ball to get to the outfielder and the distance that the outfielder has to throw the ball.

When a batter gets to first base safely, the offensive team will often use a strategy to try to get him to second. The strategies are the **steal**, the **hit-and-run**, and the **sacrifice bunt**.

## The Steal

On a steal, the runner simply starts running to the next base as the pitcher starts his pitching motion. A steal is a May Play; the runner is not forced. The fielder must physically tag the runner to get an out. The catcher will throw to the shortstop or the second baseman **covering** (standing over) second base who will try to tag the runner before the runner touches the base. If he is safe, he has stolen a base. Only fast runners regularly attempt to steal bases.

## The Sacrifice Bunt

Instead of swinging the bat, the batter sometimes holds the bat over home plate in a level position, or **squares around**, and just lets the ball hit the bat. When successfully done, the ball will roll weakly along the ground in fair territory stopping about midway between home plate and either third base or first base. This is a **bunt**.

The **sacrifice bunt** is used to advance the runner. On a good bunt, it is hard for the fielders to get a force out on the runner on second and usually easy to get the batter out at first. Think of this play as the batter 'sacrificing' his chance to get a hit, or making an out on purpose, in order to advance the runner. The play is used to get a slow runner or runner of average speed to second base. The sacrifice bunt is also very frequently used in Major League baseball when the pitcher, who is almost always a weak hitter, is at bat.

One bit of old business — it was stated earlier that with two strikes on the batter foul ground balls do not count as strike-outs, with one exception. The exception is the foul bunt. A batter who bunts a ball foul with two strikes is out on strikes.

## The Hit-and-Run

On the hit-and-run play, the runner starts running to second base just as though he was going to try to steal second base. Either the second baseman or shortstop will run over to cover the base. The batter then tries to hit the ball to the area that the shortstop or second baseman vacated.

The hit-and-run is used when the batter is good at making **contact** with the ball, meaning that he does not swing and miss very often. Generally, the runner on base must have at least average speed because, if the batter misses the ball, the runner must 'steal' second base.

**Example:** There is a runner on first. He is quite fast. The fielders are alert to the fact that he may try to steal second base. An attempted steal is when the runner begins running toward second base as soon as the pitcher starts his pitching motion. An infielder has to cover second base to receive the catcher's throw and try to physically tag out the runner. Either the second baseman or the shortstop will have to leave his normal position to cover second.

**Question:** The batter is right-handed. Which fielder will leave his position to cover second base if the runner tries to steal?

**Hint:** Remember 'pulling' the ball?

**Answer:** The second baseman. The batter may swing at the pitch. If so, he is much more likely to pull the ball to the shortstop than to the second baseman. So the shortstop should not vacate his position. Also, remember that the infielders usually 'play the batter to pull'. In other words, the infielders shift a couple steps to the right-handed batter's left. The second baseman is also closer to second base than the shortstop. For these reasons, the second baseman should cover second base with a right-handed batter at bat.

On a hit-and-run, the batter tries to hit the ball to the area that the second baseman vacated. This is the operative principle of the hit-and-run play.

How do the batter and runner know when to try the hit-and-run play? By secret **signals.** [28]

28. My friend, Susan, is critical of the fact that secret signals, attempts to intentionally upset a player's mental concentration (the brushback pitch), arguing with umpires, and standing in groups on the mound gossiping are 'part of the game'. Well, secrecy, intentional distraction, an occasional argument, and gossip are also part of her monthly bridge game. Although I grant you that scratching and spitting are not part of that tradition.

To initiate any strategy such as a hit-and-run, a bunt, or a steal, the team uses secret signals. Before the pitch, the third base coach signals to the batter and runner that the 'play' is on.

Looking at what can happen on a hit-and-run offers a good review of baseball fundamentals and the application of strategy.

Assume in these examples that there is a runner on first and no outs. The runner starts running to second as the pitcher pitches the ball to the batter. The second baseman covers second base and the right-handed batter tries to hit the ball to the area that the second baseman just vacated.

**What Can Happen on the Hit-and-Run?**

1)   The batter swings and misses.

A strike is charged to the batter. The catcher will throw to the second baseman covering second base who will try to tag the runner out. This failed hit-and-run play effectively becomes an attempted steal of second base by the runner.

2)   The batter hits the ball on the ground to the spot vacated by the second baseman. The right fielder fields it.

Fair ball hitting the ground. The batter advances to first and the runner to second.

The ball went into right field. It is obvious that the batter and runner will easily advance one base.

Once the runner tags second base he is no longer 'forced'. He may, advance as far as he dares at his own risk. With the head start that he had, he should make it easily to third base. Also note the long throw from right field to third base. Even if the runner had not had a head start, he usually has a very good chance to make it to third on a ball hit to right field.

The hit-and-run creates a hole in the infield for the batter to hit the ball through. The successful hit-and-run, at worst, leaves runners on first and third base. The batter is credited with a single in this example.

3)  The batter hits the ball on the ground right at the shortstop.

The shortstop could throw the ball to the second baseman to try to get the force out. The fielders may get a double play. But if it appears that the runner will arrive before the throw, the shortstop may throw to first to attempt to get the batter out instead. The runner, having started running when the pitch was thrown, will be much closer to second when the ball is fielded than he otherwise would have been. This brings up the disadvantage of the hit-and-run.

4)  The batter hits a fly ball or line drive that is caught.

The runner, remember, must return to tag first base after a fly ball or line drive is caught before he is allowed to advance. When a line drive is caught by an infielder the runner is partway to second base. He often won't be able to get back to first base before the infielder's throw arrives. If the fielders get the runner out at first it is a double play.

5)  The batter hits a foul ball that is not caught.

The runner returns to first base. It counts as a strike against the batter. Simple enough.

However, hitting a pitch foul on the hit-and-run play is a subtle, but important, baseball skill. Assume that the count is 2-1 on a right-handed batter. The runner has average speed. The manager 'puts the hit-and-run play on'. The batter must swing at the next pitch. The pitch is high and inside. It would be called a ball, but the batter not only has to swing at it, he must attempt to hit it to the vacated spot.

In practice, it is very difficult for the batter to hit such a pitch to the right side of the field. Therefore, the batter will intentionally attempt to hit the ball foul, or **foul off**, the pitch. The practice is called **protecting the runner**. The runner has only average speed and is likely to be thrown out at second base by the catcher if the batter did not make contact with the pitch. By fouling off the pitch, the batter 'protected' the runner from being thrown out.

◆ ◆ ◆ ◆

## Baserunning

You have already learned the most important baserunning rules — when a runner must and may try to advance. A little more detail on baserunning is needed to fully understand strategy.

First of all, with no runners on base the pitcher **winds up** before he delivers a pitch. The wind up is used to gain momentum. A right-handed pitcher, for example, places his right foot on the pitching rubber. He rocks backward one step on his left foot while swinging his arms backwards at the same time. In a smooth motion, the pitcher swings his arms above his head, then strides toward home plate with his left foot. This brings his momentum forward as he pitches the ball.

With a runner on base, the pitcher does not wind up. The base runner is allowed to stand as far away from the base as he dares while he waits for the pitcher to throw the ball. In baseball terms, he can **take a lead**.[29] Winding up would give the base runner too much time to get a head start. Instead, a right-handed pitcher, for example, stands sideways (his back to the first baseman) with his right foot on the pitching

29. In Little League baseball and slow-pitch softball the rules do not allow the runner to take a lead.

rubber and his hands together at about waist level. This is the **stretch** or **set position**. The rules require the pitcher to stand perfectly still in set position for a moment before he begins his motion to release a pitch.

While the pitcher is in the stretch position, the runner warily edges a few steps off first, or takes a lead. The first baseman stands immediately next to first base, ready for a potential throw from the pitcher. The first baseman is said to be **holding the runner on base**. Instead of throwing a pitch to the batter, the pitcher can throw to the first baseman who attempts to tag the runner with the ball before he gets back to the base. Such throws to first are called **pickoff throws**. The **pickoff play** is a May Play, of course. The pitcher can stand still in the stretch position for as long as he wants. There is no limit to the number of throws that the pitcher can make to a base in an attempt to pickoff a runner.

It was stated earlier that, on a sacrifice bunt, it is much easier to get the batter out than the runner. That's because the runner takes a lead, or has a head start.

A runner needs to get a good running start on a steal or a hit-and-run play. The runner will take a lead and start running at the instant that he is certain that the pitcher is going to throw a pitch. If he starts too early, he may be picked off.

## How Signals Work

Offensive plays are transmitted to the batter and runner by secret, coded signals. The batter and runner(s) know whether a hit-and-run play is in effect, for example, by reading signals.

How do signals work?

You have probably seen a batter lingering idly about home plate and looking around the field with a blank, glazed expression. This is invariably the moment when my girlfriend looks up from her book, thinking as follows: "Baseball again (sigh). How can they (ResBexes) watch this hour after hour? I wonder what else is on TV." She gives me a sideways glance and lowers her eyes to her book. I know that she is making a mental note that I owe her a favor for monopolizing the TV. Again.[30]

Before she read this, she was not aware of the subtleties of the sport. The batter, and any runner on base, is looking at the third base coach who is giving them signals or **signs**. The coach stands in foul territory near third base.

He signals by gesturing busily, like a person who went camping in the deep woods without mosquito repellant. For example, the coach may, in rapid succession, brush his hand across his chest, brush his thigh, take off his hat and wipe his forehead, clap his hands, and, of course, he will generally spit and 'scratch himself'. The signals work like the game 'Simon Says' except that only one of them means "*Simon says* 'Do this'!" The rest of the gestures are meaningless and used only to make it more difficult for the other team to break the code or **steal the signs**. The sign that means "Simon says 'Do This'," is the **indicator**. Assume that the sign for the indicator is brushing a hand across the chest. The very next sign will tell the batter and runner what to do.

You are the batter. Grabbing the belt is the hit-and-run sign. If the coach brushes his thigh, takes his hat off, claps his hands, brushes his chest, grabs his belt, claps his hands again, scratches, and spits, it means?

30. After you have known someone for a number of years sometimes certain conversations seem superfluous.

It means that the hit-and-run play is on. You must swing at the next pitch. The runner will be running to second base.

These signals tell players what strategy is in effect or, in baseball slang, whether a **play is on**. The above example illustrates just one way of giving signs. There are many others.[31]

How does the third base coach know when to signal a play?

The manager signals to him.

31. When a runner gets to first base in Little League, the coach may just holler to him, "Go [steal second] on the first pitch." Higher levels of baseball require more secrecy.

# How To Use Your Players

Use of strategy depends on the score, the inning, the number of outs, and the abilities of the players — particularly the batter and pitcher. Some strategy involves putting a play on (hit-and-run, steal, sacrifice bunt). However, strategy also means playing smart or players properly exercising their own discretion on the field. There are certain things that a player should always do and certain things that he should never do. Now that you understand the fundamentals — what a player may or must do — you will easily understand the reasons that a player should or should not do the following.

## Always Do's and Never Do's

### The Pitcher — Always Do

It bears repeating that a pitcher should attempt to stay ahead of the batter in the count. The counts of 0-1, 1-2, and 0-2, clearly favor the pitcher. When the pitcher is ahead in the count, he can throw any type of pitch. The batter does not have the luxury of guessing that he will throw a particular pitch because if the batter guesses wrong he will fall further behind in the count (or, if he has two strikes, he will strike out). On the other hand when the pitcher falls behind in the count, he needs a strike. The pitcher often throws a fastball because it's the easiest pitch to throw accurately. It's also the easiest pitch to hit.

### The Pitcher — Never Do

The pitcher should never walk the first batter in an inning. When he receives a walk, the lead off batter has an excellent chance to score because he has three outs to travel around the bases. He may try to steal or may advance into scoring position on a base hit, or on an out, such as a sacrifice bunt or slowly hit ground ball. Even the best hitters are successful in getting a hit only once in every three tries. Therefore, the pitcher should always try to make the lead off batter hit the ball to get on base. For example, the pitcher may throw more fastballs in order to get ahead in the count.

### The Batter — Always Do

With two strikes a batter should always swing at a pitch that is close to the strike zone or **close pitch**. The umpire is not perfect; he may call a pitch a strike even though it is not in the strike zone.

### The Batter — Never Do

A batter with a 3-0 count should never swing at a ball outside the strike zone. Unless the pitcher throws a strike the batter gets a walk. The batter is way ahead on the count and should only swing at a 3-0 pitch that he thinks he can hit well. The batter generally guesses that a fastball will be thrown in a certain area of the strike zone, such as the inside half of the plate. He prepares to hit that pitch and should not swing at any other pitch. If the pitcher throws a strike over the outside corner — a difficult pitch to hit well — the batter should take the pitch. Only a small advantage is gained by the pitcher.

### The Runner — Always Do

With two outs, a runner (or runners) always should begin running as soon as the batter hits the pitch. The runner has everything to gain and nothing to lose.

Assume that a runner is on second base and the batter hits a fly ball that should be an easy catch for the fielder. The runner should start running. If the fielder catches the ball, the inning is over anyway.[32] The runner will score if the fielder fails to catch the ball.

One common sense exception to this 'Always Do' is that an unforced runner should not run when he would be likely to be tagged for the third out.

### The Runner — Never Do

With less than two outs, a runner should never run on a line drive that might be caught by an infielder. He should wait to see whether the ball hits the ground. If he starts running, and an infielder catches the line drive, then the runner probably will not be able to get back to the base before the infielder's throw to the fielder covering the base. If the ball **goes through** (hits the ground and travels into the outfield) the runner will advance easily anyway. A runner on third will score on any ball that goes through. He gains nothing with a head start.

### The Fielders — 'Almost' Always Do

Fielders have 'almost always do's'. The batter, runner(s), and pitcher are the protagonists of the action. The fielders react to what they do. What fielders should do is dictated by game situation and players' abilities, the inning, the score, and the number of outs, and the speed of the batter and/or runner, and where and how hard the ball is hit.

Generally, with no outs an infielder should (almost) always get the **lead runner** out when he can do so easily. The lead runner is the runner who has made the most progress around the bases. Assume there are no outs and men on first and second. A ground ball is hit at the third

---

32. Remember, if the batter or a runner is out on a Must Play, a runner does not score a run even if he crosses home plate before the out is made.

baseman. The third baseman should tag third base for the force out. Then he can throw to first base for an attempted double play. He should take the force out at third even though he may have a good chance to get a double play by relaying the ball to second base. (The second baseman would, of course, then relay the ball to first.) It is preferable to take the lead runner off the bases than to risk a wild throw or a runner being safe on an attempted double play. By getting the lead runner out, the defensive team avoids the possibility of having a runner on third with less than two outs. A runner can score from third base with less than two outs in many ways.

### The Fielders — Never do

The following is a short list of types of fielding mistakes. These mistakes are commonly seen at nonprofessional levels of baseball.

A fielder should never make an unnecessary throw. He should hold the ball instead of risking a wild throw when he has no real chance to get an out or the runner will not be able to advance anyway. Assume that there is a runner on third base with no outs. The batter hits a pop fly which the shortstop catches in shallow left field. The runner will not try to advance. Instead of throwing to home plate, the shortstop should run into the infield and give the ball to the pitcher. This practice is known as **running the ball in**.

A fielder should not **throw** (the ball) **behind the runner**. Assume the batter hits a ball into the gap in left-center field. The batter will easily get to second base. If the left fielder throws to second base, the runner may be able to advance to third base during the time it takes for the throw to get to second base. The left fielder should throw to third base in order to keep the runner at second base.

The fielders should never leave a base uncovered when a runner may advance to that base. The infielders rotate in different ways to ensure that the necessary bases are covered. Assume that there are no outs and no one on base. The batter hits a fair ball that rolls down the right field foul line. The batter tries for a double. The right fielder's throw to second base is off line and rolls through the infield between the pitcher's mound and third base. The third baseman should not retrieve the ball. He would leave third base uncovered if he did. The pitcher, catcher, or other fielder should retrieve the errant throw.

The better players are **fundamentally sound**, meaning that they execute routine plays and basic skills well. As important as physical skill is the avoidance of **mental mistakes**. Violation of the Always Do's and Never Do's are mental mistakes.

## Types of Pitchers

In the last chapter you will manage a team. The first thing a manager needs to know is how to use his pitchers.

There are two main categories of pitcher: the **starting pitcher** and the **relief pitcher**.

A Major League team will usually have five starting pitchers. These pitchers take turns starting games. Smith starts game one, Jones starts game two, etc. Pitching puts severe stress on the arm so a starting pitcher needs a few days rest between starts to recover. The manager usually hopes that the starter will be able to pitch at least six or seven innings. A starting pitcher may pitch the entire game but starters infrequently pitch **complete games**.

A starting pitcher will be removed from a game by the manager if he is pitching badly or his arm tires. Sometimes a starting pitcher will also be removed late in the game, even though he is pitching well, in order to substitute a **pinch hitter** for him. A pinch hitter is a player who bats in the place of the pitcher (or any player). In the Major Leagues, pinch hitters are substitute position players.

When the starting pitcher is removed a relief pitcher takes over pitching duties. The age of specialization has affected baseball — there are three types of relief pitchers. The **long reliever**, also known as the **middle reliever** because he pitches the middle innings of the game, the **short reliever**, who pitches in the late innings, and the **closer**, who gets the last outs in the game.

In the Major Leagues, long relief pitchers are usually journeyman pitchers who have had moderate success or are young pitchers who have not proven themselves. Middle relievers pitch the less critical part of the game, the middle innings. These poor souls are frequently brought in to pitch when the game is out of hand; the other team has scored early and often on the starter.

The short relief man only pitches an inning or two or pitches only to certain batters. For instance, a right-handed short relief pitcher will usually be brought into the game to pitch to a right-handed batter. Remember that the 'same-handedness' advantage goes to the pitcher. Short relievers are ordinarily brought into close games in the seventh, eighth, or ninth innings. Although they usually pitch two innings or less a short reliever may be required to pitch in two or three consecutive games.

When his team is ahead in the last inning of a close game the manager will bring in his best short relief man, or closer, to close out the game.

The closer typically throws very hard, mainly fastballs and sliders. The closer is often brought into the game when runners are on base. His role is to strike-out batters.

Parenthetically, you have seen play stopped while the infielders converge on the mound where they stand around chatting. The players sometimes cover their mouths as they talk, lending an air of conspiracy to the meeting.

What the heck are they talking about?

They are discussing strategy or just killing time. Players need to kill time in order to give a relief pitcher time to warm up before he enters the game. To warm up, the reliever throws practice pitches in a designated area off the playing field. Sometimes he has to come in on short notice. After the players have yakked for a minute or so the manager makes a slow walk to the mound to dismiss the pitcher and call-in the reliever.

To kill time in the old days (about twenty-some years ago), Major League players would discuss hunting and fishing plans. Now they discuss golf and investments. The average Major League salary is $1,000,000.00 per year.

Like scratching and spitting, killing time is an old baseball tradition. And, as baseball custom, the umpires will allow the players a couple of minutes to purportedly discuss strategy although he knows that the players are simply delaying. The delays are infrequent and brief. But now you understand that there is a reason for this pokiness.

## Statistics

A player's individual offensive and defensive statistics are rough measures of his ability. Statistics are used in virtually every strategy decision.

The batter's batting average is the percentage of **at bats** in which he gets a hit. The pitcher gives up an average of so many runs per game.

Baseball lends itself to compilation of individual statistics more easily than any other sport. In football or basketball the outcome of each play is a result of the joint and simultaneous efforts of all the players on the offense and defense. Reliable individual statistics cannot be developed for these sports. In baseball, on the other hand, each play is easily categorized based on what that player does with the ball. The pitcher is wholly responsible for what happens to his pitches, the batter for where he hits the ball (or if he doesn't hit the ball), and the fielder for what he does with balls hit or thrown to him. Each play is a discrete, individual event.

The best known and most useful statistic in baseball is batting average. Recall that batting average is the percentage of at bats in which the batter gets a hit or total hits divided by total at bats. Walks, successful sacrifice bunts, and sacrifice flies do not count as an official at bat when figuring batting average. That is because a base on balls is a neutral event, not the result of a batted ball. The sacrifice bunt and sacrifice fly are not counted as it is deemed that the batter was intentionally giving up his chance to get a hit in order to advance the runner. Any kind of a hit, whether it's a single, double, triple, or home run, counts as one hit.

The figure for batting average is carried out to three decimal places. Major League batting averages are mentioned by a radio or television announcer almost every time that the player comes to bat and are listed in the Sunday sports pages. An average of .300 (pronounced "three hundred") or above is the mark of a superior hitter. The best batting average in Major League baseball is usually around .350. No one has hit .400 for 50 years. A batting average of .250 denotes an average hitter and about .220 and under is the mark of a poor hitter.[33]

The total number of home runs that a batter hits and the number of runners that score as a result of a batter's hit are also important statistics. Batters who get a lot of **extra base hits** – doubles and home runs – are power hitters.

The batter gets credit for a **run batted in** or **RBI** when a runner scores as a result of the batter's batted ball.

Example: Assume that there are runners on second and third base. The batter hits a single to left field. Both the runners both score. The batter gets credit for two RBI's.

Example: Assume that there is a runner on third base with one out. The batter hits a sacrifice fly to right field. A sacrifice fly, of course, means that the runner tags up and scores after the catch. The batter gets credit for one RBI.

Example: There is a runner on third base with one out. The batter hits a slow ground ball to the shortstop. The runner scores and the batter is out at first base. The batter gets credit for an RBI.

Example: There are runners on first and second base. The batter hits a home run. The batter is credited with three RBI's. The batter is credited with one RBI for the run that he scores himself as well as one RBI for each runner on base.

A batter is not credited with an RBI if a run scores when he hits into a double play. He is credited with one RBI if he walks with the bases loaded. When a batter walks with the bases loaded, each runner advances one base. The runner who was on third base scores a run.

33. The lower the level of the league, the higher batting averages tend to be. It's not uncommon for some Little Leaguers to hit .500.

While all players will have some RBI's, the team's power hitters usually 'drive in' the most runs. However, most power hitters also strike out more frequently than other batters. This is so because a power hitter generally swings the bat in a longer arc in order to increase bat speed. Therefore, he has a lesser chance to hit the ball than a batter who waits until the last instant before triggering a short, compact swing. The batter who waits longer before triggering the swing will be better able to judge the final location of the pitch than a batter who starts his swing earlier.

For pitchers, **earned run average** or **ERA** is the traditional measure of ability. ERA is the average number of runs that a pitcher gives up per nine innings. A pitcher who allows a runner or runners to get on base is charged with any runs that these runners score. Assume that Adams pitches to two batters in an inning, both of whom get on base with hits. Adams is then removed from the game. Relief pitcher Bonner comes into the game. If either or both of the runners score — while Bonner is pitching — then the run or runs scored count against Adams for purposes of figuring ERA.

Runs scored by runners who score as a result of an error or who get on base because of an error, are **unearned runs**. Unearned runs are not counted when figuring a pitcher's earned run average. Remember that an error is a fielder's flub or misplay. Some examples of errors are a fly ball that a player drops, a routine ground ball that an infielder doesn't field cleanly which results in the batter being safe and a wild throw by a fielder that enables a runner to advance an 'extra' base (one more base than he should have been able to advance).

As with batting average, three is also the magic number for an ERA. Any number below 3.00 is an excellent ERA, below 3.50 is good, while an ERA above 4.00 is poor.

Each pitcher also has a **won-lost record**. Several pitchers may pitch for each team in a single game. One pitcher on the winning team will get credit for the **win** and one pitcher on the losing team will be charged with the **loss**. The winning pitcher is the pitcher who is in the game when his team last takes the lead. The losing pitcher is the pitcher who gives up that lead. A pitcher is charged with a loss for allowing the runner who scores the 'winning' run to get on base. For example, assume that the TigerCat-Otter game ends 5-3 in favor of the Otters. The TigerCat pitcher who allowed the runner who scored the Otters' fourth run *to get on base* is the losing pitcher. He is the losing pitcher even if the run was unearned or another pitcher was in the game at the time that the runner scored. However, a starting pitcher must pitch five full innings to qualify for a win. A relief pitcher, on the other hand, could throw one pitch and get the win or the loss. A win-loss record of 15-12 means that a pitcher was credited with 15 wins and charged with 12 losses. Wins are always stated first.

In this information age, everything that is quantifiable in a baseball game has a statistical category. All this information can be retrieved instantaneously from computers. Some Major League baseball managers use computers to plan strategy against a particular opponent. However, batting average and earned run average are the traditional measures of performance.

While it is true that baseball events are neatly quantifiable there are some variables in comparing players. Because a pitcher on Team A has an ERA of 3.10 does not necessarily mean that he is better than a pitcher on Team B who has an ERA of 3.40. The pitchers' hometown ballparks, where they play one-half their games, may be very different. One ballpark may have a shorter distance to the outfield fences than another. What would be a home run in Ballpark B might be caught for an out in larger Ballpark A. The amount of foul area is important. The more foul area, the more opportunity the defense has to catch a foul fly for an out. The ability of the defensive players is very important. Maybe players on Team A cover more area or have better **range**. They are able to get outs on what would be hits if Team B was in the field. A pitcher also can have one or two horrible innings that will skew his ERA. Statistics are just good estimates of ability, not an exact science.

### Talking Baseball

Comparison of player statistics is an interesting and essential part of talking baseball. For example Major League fans and sportswriters compare players on different teams when a team is considering trading one or more of its players for one or more of another team's players. Assume that the Otters appear to have a championship caliber team except that they need a power hitter. Should the Otters trade young pitcher Jones, who has good potential, for the TigerCats' established, but long-in-the-tooth power hitter Smith? Smith's home run total declined last year. Was it merely an off year or have his skills eroded? If the trade is made, the results are hashed over during and at the end of the season and, sometimes, for years afterward. Especially if pitcher Jones eventually realizes his potential and power hitter Smith does not perform up to expectations, denying the Otters a championship.

"I don't know why they traded Jones for that bum, Smith," Otter fans (even those who were in favor of the trade) will say righteously for years after the trade.

Now you are talking baseball.

### Test Your Statistics IQ

**Question**: Why do closers usually have lower ERA's than starters?

Your ResBex will not get the answer easily. This challenging question requires you to apply your baseball expertise. But if you simply understand the answer then you have a very good grasp of statistics.

**Answer:** The closer's usual role is to enter a game in the ninth inning when his team has a lead. Often there are one or more outs and one or more runners on base when he comes in. Assume that the Otters are at bat in the bottom of the ninth with one out and the bases loaded. The TigerCats are ahead by one run. The TigerCat closer is brought in. The batter hits a double. Two runners score. The game is over. The runs are charged to the previous pitcher (or pitchers) who put the scoring runners on base. Often the winning run or runs will not be charged to the closer even though he gave up the hit that allowed them to score!

Also, with one or two outs there is less chance that the batter or batters that the closer pitches to — whose runs would count against the closer's ERA — will score. On the other hand, a team that is behind by a run with no outs in the ninth inning will often use the sacrifice bunt to get a runner to second base. They will give the closer an out! Also, the fielders have a better chance to get an out or a double play when there are runners on base (who would be forced on a ground ball).

That's why the ERA of most closers, or short relievers in general, will be lower than the ERA of a starter.

Now you are really talking baseball. The next chapter will polish up some fine points. Then you will be managing the TigerCats in the pivotal Cats-Otters game.

# A Little More Offensive Strategy and How to Defeat It

This chapter covers other routine baseball practices that you will observe during a game. It also tops off your baseball knowledge with very important bits of strategy, particularly late game, or 'late inning,' strategies.

## The Runner

### Overrunning First Base

A batter is allowed to overrun first base after hitting a ball. For example, assume that the batter hits a ground ball to the shortstop. The batter runs full speed to beat the throw to first base. He does not have to stop on the base. The rules allow the batter to tag first base and continue past it in foul territory until his momentum stops. If the batter is called safe on the play, he returns to occupy first base. However, a runner is not allowed to overrun second or third base. He can be tagged out by fielders if he does.[34] A runner overruns first base when he is not going to try to advance farther on the batted ball.

### Sliding

So what does a runner do when he needs to come to a sudden stop at second base, third base or home plate? He **slides** to a stop. Most players slide feet first (on their hip), some slide head first (on their

---

34. Of course, the runner can just tag and overrun home plate. A runner cannot occupy home plate.

stomach). While the purpose of a slide is simply to stop on the base, a skillful runner will slide away from a fielder's attempted tag.

One of a forced runner's duties on a ground ball is to **break up the** (attempted) **double play** by sliding. This is one of the few plays in which contact is permitted. Here is why. Assume a runner is on first with one out. The batter hits a ground ball to the shortstop. The shortstop throws to the second baseman. The second baseman receiving the ball must, after tagging second base, pivot to throw to first base. On a close play, the second baseman's front foot will be in the runner's path to second base. Even though he is out, the runner still has to stop his own momentum. It is traditional for the runner to attempt to make contact with the fielder in order to disrupt his throw to first base. [35]

### Blocking Bases

A fielder in possession of the ball may attempt to **block** a base with his body. Generally fielders do not do so because the players in higher leagues wear sharp metal spikes on the bottom of their shoes. However, the catcher, who wears protective padding, will often block home plate. Note: The catcher must have possession of the ball (or be in the act of catching it) before he may attempt to block home plate. The runner is allowed to run into the catcher to attempt to dislodge the ball. [36]

35. The runner is not permitted to simply slide into the fielder in order to interfere with him while making no attempt to slide into the base. If the runner does so, the runner and the batter will both be called out because of the runner's interference.

36. Generally, at levels of baseball below the college level, the rules require a runner to slide in order to avoid, or minimize, contact with the fielder.

## Getting a Good Jump

When a steal or a hit-and-run play is in effect the runner starts running as the ball is pitched instead of waiting for the batter to hit the ball.  On such plays, the runner is said to be **going on the pitch**, or **going**. It is important for the runner to get a good start toward second base. A runner does so by starting for second base at precisely the instant that the pitcher begins his *pitching* motion. Getting a good start is called getting a **good jump** on the pitch.

On most pitches no strategy will be in effect. The runner will always take a lead, though, to get a head start in the event of a batted ball or wild pitch.

## Going Halfway

When he is not forced, the runner uses his own judgment as to whether he should run on a batted ball. Assume that a runner is on second with no outs. The batter hits a fly ball to left field. It appears that the left fielder will catch the ball. The runner goes part of the way to third base and waits to see if the outfielder catches the ball. If the outfielder catches the ball, the runner retreats to second base.  He will only venture far enough off second base that he is sure that he will be able to get back to second base safely before the fielder's throw if the fielder catches the ball. If the fielder drops the ball, the runner has a head start. This technique is called **going halfway**. If a runner intended to tag up on a fly ball, he would have been standing on second base waiting for the catch to be made.

## The Third Base Coach: A Traffic Light for Runners

Sometimes the runner loses sight of the ball as he travels around the bases. On these plays, the third base coach acts as a traffic light telling him whether to go or stop.

You are on first. The batter hits a ball that falls in the gap between the right fielder and the center fielder and rolls to the outfield wall. You see that you will be able to make it to third easily; you may even be able to score. As you approach third base, the ball is behind you. You cannot judge whether you have a good chance to score. You focus on your third base coach. He will signal you to 'go home' or stop at third.

# The Fielders

With no one on base, fielders position themselves where they think the batter is most likely to hit the ball. We know that a batter generally pulls the ball and that fielders take a couple of steps to a right-handed batter's left or a couple steps to a left-handed batter's right. Fielders will also position themselves in certain ways to limit a base runner's advance or to attempt to defeat an expected offensive strategy.

## The Relay Throw

There is a runner on first base. The batter hits a ball in the gap between the right and center fielder. The ball rolls to the wall. The runner is roaring past second base. Meanwhile, the right fielder has retrieved the ball. As the runner approaches third base, he sees his coach frantically windmilling his arms, signalling him to score. The right fielder heaves the ball to his second baseman who is standing in the outfield about fifteen feet behind the infield dirt. The second baseman, in turn, throws the ball to the catcher.

On this play, the second baseman is the **relay man**. He relays the ball to the catcher. The relay is used when the ball must travel a long distance.

## The Cut Off Throw

Teams often **concede the run** in the early innings, in order to attempt to limit the damage or prevent the batter from getting into scoring position. For example, when a runner will easily score on a single into the outfield, the outfielder will merely throw the ball into second base. Why risk an unnecessary throw?

However, on balls in which the fielder has a good chance to throw the runner out at home, the fielder can have it both ways. He can attempt to throw the runner out and hold the batter at first base. The fielders do so by using the **cut off throw**.

There is a runner on second and the batter hits a hard line drive which bounces in front of the left fielder. The third baseman positions himself about midway between third base and home plate, in line with the left fielder and the catcher. If the left fielder's throw arrives before the runner, the third baseman will let it go. The catcher will receive the ball and attempt to tag out the runner. On the other hand, if the throw is too late to get the runner out then the third baseman cut offs, or catches, the throw. Then, the third baseman is in position to throw out the batter at second base if he tries to advance. The third baseman is the **cut off man**.

The first baseman is usually the cut off man on balls hit to right and center field. The third baseman is the cut off man on balls hit to left field. The cut off man functions as a kind of quality control inspector, catching any throw that will be too late or is off target. The catcher always has the play in front of him. His job is to yell "Cut!" on late or bad throws.

More generally, a cut off man is any player positioned to catch a bad throw from the outfield before it reaches its destination in order to limit the batter's advance.

### Positioning to Defend the Sacrifice Bunt

Assume that a man is on first with no outs. The fielders suspect that a sacrifice bunt attempt is in the works. If the batter bunts, the fielders want to get a force out on the runner at second base. The faster a fielder can get to the expected bunt the better chance he will have to get an out. Therefore, the third baseman will position himself on the infield grass just in front of the dirt portion of the infield. He is said to be **playing in on the grass** or **playing in**. He will take a few more steps toward home when the pitch is released.

The fielders also attempt to keep the runner close to first base. For this reason, the first baseman must remain at first base or 'hold the runner on'. As the pitcher releases the pitch, the first baseman and the third baseman charge toward home plate to get in closer to a potential bunt. Of course, the weakness of the defense is that the batter may swing. The first and third basemen would have little time to react to a ball hit in their direction. The positioning of their first and third basemen is called **playing in at the corners**. It is the standard defense for a sacrifice bunt.

If the first baseman is charging home plate, who covers first base (to get the batter out) in the event that the batter bunts?

The second baseman covers first base and the shortstop covers second base.

### Playing the Infield In

**Example:** The game is tied. There is a man on third and no outs in the bottom half of the ninth inning. One run will win the game. How do the fielders position themselves?

**Answer:** All the infielders play in on the infield grass, It's called **playing the infield in.** In this way, the infielders have a much better chance of throwing out the runner at home on a ground ball. By playing the infield in, the infielders have less range or a lesser chance of getting to a ground ball. But getting the batter out is irrelevant; if the runner scores the game is over. The fielders will only attempt to get the batter out if they can also prevent the run from scoring.[37] Of course, the runner will score on a hit or a sacrifice fly, error, wild pitch, and perhaps on a slow ground ball.

# The Batter

### You Think You've Got Stress: The Squeeze Play

A runner on third base with less than two outs has a high likelihood of scoring a run because he can score on a hit or on certain types of outs or even when there is no batted ball. The runner could score on a slow ground ball, or a hard-hit ground ball that requires an infielder to make a pivot to throw to home plate, a sacrifice fly, a wild pitch, etc.

One important play falls under 'etc.' — the **squeeze**. The **squeeze play** is simply a bunt with a runner on third. There are two types of squeeze — the dramatic **suicide squeeze** and the **safety squeeze**. On a suicide squeeze the runner 'goes' on the pitch as if he is stealing home.[38] The batter bunts the ball. As a practical matter, the runner will always score on any fair bunted ball that hits the ground. Always. If the batter misses the ball or a bunted ball is caught in the air, the runner will be out (with rare exception). He's dead. Thus, the name suicide. It's a do-or-die play. The pressure is on the batter to **get the ball down** (on the ground) in fair territory.

37. When the game is in the last inning and one run would win the game, the outfielders will also move closer to the infield or 'play shallow'. In this way, the outfielder may catch a line drive that would otherwise drop for a single.

38. A runner can attempt to steal home. His chances of success will depend on whether he gets a good jump, his speed, the speed of the pitch, and where the catcher catches the ball.

On a safety squeeze, the runner does not go on the pitch. Instead, he waits to see where the batter bunts the ball, then decides whether he will try to score. The fielders may have a chance to get the runner out if he decides to try to score.

# The Pitcher

### Keeping the Runner Close (to his base)

A major duty of the pitcher is to **hold a runner close** to his base. The pitcher does so by throwing over to the fielder covering the base as the runner takes his lead. Pitchers try to be deceptive, or not tip off the runner, when they are going to throw to a base instead of throwing a pitch.[39] Even if the pitcher is unsuccessful in picking off the runner, his pickoff throws keep the runner closer to the base by disrupting his timing.

A pitcher who can effectively disguise when he is going to throw to first base and makes pickoff throws with a quick motion is said to have a **good move**. When he suspects that a steal or hit-and-run play is on,

39. Another footnote for the benefit of picky ResBexes: Technically (very technically), it is a violation of the rules for a pitcher to use a motion that will intentionally deceive a runner. Such deception is called a **balk**. When the umpire calls a balk, each runner is allowed to advance one base. When a pitcher makes a motion which is consistent with pitching (throwing to home plate) and makes a pickoff throw instead, he balks. If the pitcher does not step directly toward a base when trying a pickoff throw, he balks. Balk calls are usually very subtle rule interpretations in Major League baseball. I think umpires take the "I can't define it but I know it when I see it" viewpoint. Anyway, if and when you understand this rule, call me.

the pitcher will almost always throw to first base at least once to keep the runner close to the base.

## The Pitchout

Certain pitches counter offensive strategy. High pitches are harder to bunt than low pitches. An inside pitch is hard for a batter to hit to the vacated area on a hit-and-run. And then there's the **pitchout**.

The pitchout is just a fast pitch thrown chest high about a foot-and-a-half outside home plate. The catcher jumps out to the side to catch it. The batter cannot reach it with his bat. If the hit-and-run is in effect when a pitchout is thrown, the base runner is usually a dead duck because the batter cannot hit the ball. Such a pitch makes it easier for the catcher to throw out the runner; the pitch gets to the catcher quickly and, because he does not have to rise out of his crouch, he is already standing in position to throw when he catches the ball. For this reason, the pitchout is also effective against the straight steal.

The manager signals to his catcher and pitcher when he wants a pitchout. He tries to guess on which pitch in the count the team at bat will try a steal or hit-and-run. The pitchout will be called a 'ball', of course.

## Be My Guest: The Intentional Walk

Another pitcher's strategy is the **intentional walk**. This is a very important late-inning strategy. The intentional walk is just what it sounds like; the pitcher lobs four pitches well outside home plate. In this manner, the pitcher intentionally gives the batter a base on balls.

There are two reasons this play is used. One reason is to create a force play. Assume the game is tied in the bottom of the ninth inning. One run will win the game. There is one out and a man on second. The team in the field intentionally walks the batter. Now there are men on first and second, which means that on a ground ball there will be a force play at second and third base (as well as the play at first base). The intentional walk increases the fielders' chances of getting a force out and, by putting a man on first base, creates the possibility of a double play if the batter hits a ground ball to an infielder. A double play would end the inning. Nothing is lost by walking the batter. If the runner on second scores the game is over anyway. A run scored by the batter who was intentionally walked would mean nothing.

The team in the field will also intentionally walk an excellent hitter in certain late-inning situations. They will walk an excellent hitter when there is an unoccupied base behind the lead runner and one run will win the game. Assume that the game is tied. There are runners on first and third. Your best hitter is at bat. The other team will often intentionally walk him (loading the bases) since the run that he might score would be meaningless. The other team will make you beat them with a lesser hitter.

**Example:** You manage the visiting TigerCats. The team is in the field. It is a tie game. There is one out and a man on third in the last half of the ninth inning. 'Sweet Lou' Sims is up. Sweet Lou is an excellent contact hitter, meaning that he swings and misses very infrequently. His batting-average is .335. The batter after Sims is Kal 'K.O.' Kline. K.O. has a batting average of .265. He hits a lot of home runs, but he also strikes out a lot. What are you going to do?

**Answer:** Walk 'Sweet Lou'. The chances are great that he will at least hit the ball somewhere, possibly scoring the run. Remember all the ways that a runner can score from third base with less than two outs. Intentionally putting Lou on first base sets up the potential (ground ball) double play that would end the inning.

Also, K.O. may strike out. His ability to hit for power doesn't mean anything because just a single will win the game for the Otters. When a single will beat your team, you would certainly rather pitch to a .265 hitter than a .335 hitter. For these reasons, the manager would rather pitch to K.O. in this situation than Sweet Lou.

◆ ◆ ◆ ◆

There are certain 'little' things that players should do. Here is an illustration of 'unseen' baseball strategy that incorporates batting and pitching strategy.

## A Subtle Strategy: Hitting Behind the Runner

**Example:** The game is in the fourth inning, there is a man on second with no outs. The batter is one of your team's better hitters. He is right-handed as is the pitcher. You want to try to get the runner to third base because a runner on third base with one out has an excellent chance to score. On the other hand, you would like to let the batter try to get a hit instead of having him bunt the runner to third. A single to the outfield will probably score the runner.

What can the batter do to both try to get a hit and increase the runner's chances to advance even if he is unsuccessful?

**Answer:** You can have your cake and eat it, too. The batter can try to hit the ball to the right side of the field or the opposite field. If he gets a hit, the runner will probably score. If the batter hits a ground ball to the right side of the infield, the runner should be able to advance to third base. If the batter hits a fly ball to the right fielder, the runner should be able to tag up and advance to third base (because of the long throw). The odds are very high that a ball hit to the right side (other than a pop-up) will at least move the runner to third base, if not score him.

Of course, hitting the ball to right field is not natural for a right-handed batter. He would normally pull the ball to the left side of the field. To try to hit the ball to the right side of the field, a right-handed batter must adjust his swing a little bit. The practice of intentionally trying to hit the ball to right field with a runner on second base is called **hitting behind the runner**. A left-handed batter naturally hits behind the runner.

Remember, a single into the outfield would score the run and the batter is always at a disadvantage when batting with two strikes. Therefore, the batter is generally willing to use just the first strike to try to hit to right field. After that he will just try to get a hit anywhere.

Which pitch does a right-handed batter hit best to the opposite field? A pitch on the outside part of the plate.

### *Foiling Offensive Strategy*

That's where the pitcher will probably try to throw the ball anyway, right? — on the outside part of the plate?

Not necessarily. Knowing that the right-handed batter will probably try to hit to the opposite field, the pitcher may try to throw a high inside strike. This pitch is the most difficult for the batter to hit to the right side (it's in his 'pull' zone). Therefore, it would be the best pitch to defeat the strategy.

Such a pitch is often one of the tense moments in a baseball game. The pitcher may have just an average fastball. Should he attempt to get the fastball high and inside where the batter may pull it or stay with his best pitch — the curveball. There is no guarantee that the batter will be trying to hit behind the runner. The batter may *pull* the fastball instead. Now you should be getting the feel of the game. A single pitch can be very important.

# Now You Know Baseball

Whether you decide to try to answer the strategy questions in the following chapters or just read through them, you know baseball if you understand the explanation in the answers. This section synopsizes baseball strategy.

Traditionally, baseball strategy is used sparingly and only when the odds of success are favorable. Using strategy in this manner is called **playing by the book**. The venerable, fictitious 'book' is a compilation of baseball wisdom over the ages. For example, using a left-handed relief pitcher to pitch to a left-handed batter and not requiring the team's best hitters to bunt are examples of playing by the book. A manager is almost always better served by playing it by the book. On the other hand, making too many strategy moves is called **overmanaging**. Overmanaging will lose more games than it wins. It's a long season. The manager is less essential to the success of the team than the player. A good manager lets the players win or lose the games.

## The Two Rules of Managing

Deciding on whether to use a particular strategy is a two-step process. First, consider viable strategies. *When considering strategy, you should always look two batters ahead in the batting order*. For example, you should not use a sacrifice bunt when one of the next two batters will be your pitcher (assuming that you will not be pinch hitting for your pitcher). Pitchers are, of course, notoriously weak hitters. The purpose of the sacrifice bunt is to move a runner into scoring position in order to give two good hitters the chance to get the hit that will score him. Another age-old baseball saying is that even the best hitters are successful only three times in every ten tries. Remember that a batting average of .300 is the mark of an excellent hitter. Therefore, for the runner on second base to have a better than even chance to score, you need to have a couple of average-to-good hitters due to bat.

*The second step is to consider what the other team may do to counter your strategy.* Assume that the game is in the bottom of the ninth inning. Your lead-off batter singles. Now you have the potential winning run on first base with no outs. You successfully sacrifice the runner to second base. Your best hitter is due to bat. Well, the other team will intentionally walk your best hitter. A sacrifice bunt is not necessarily a bad move in that situation. It gets the runner into scoring position. But a batter other than your best hitter will have to drive him in. Always consider what the other team will do.

## The Early Innings and The Late Innings

For strategy purposes, a baseball game has two parts — the early innings and the late innings. The seventh inning is the beginning of the late innings. In the early innings, teams simply try to score as many runs as possible. The manager generally uses only obvious strategy. For example with a runner on first base with less than two outs and the pitcher at bat, the manager will almost always use the sacrifice bunt. The steal and hit-and-run will be used in appropriate situations but, for the most part, the manager lets the hitters hit. He does not risk making outs.[40]

In the late innings — the seventh, eighth, and ninth innings — the manager generally has to make personnel changes such as using relief

40. Strategy is used at the manager's discretion. A manager, depending on his personnel and his managing style, may prefer to risk outs (use strategy) in order to get ahead early in the game. However, the 'book' dictates that a manager use strategy conservatively in the early innings.

pitchers and pinch hitters. The manager may use the hit-and-run, the sacrifice bunt, and the steal to try to score one run in the late innings.

Often, there is no 'right' choice of strategy. A couple of different strategies, or using no strategy at all, may be equally good choices. At the risk of stating the obvious — success depends on how well the players execute the strategy. You know the basic strategies but, before you put on the manager's cap, let's take a look at when to use them.

### The Hit-and-Run, The Steal, and The Sacrifice Bunt Redux

You should consider the use of offensive strategy from a cost-benefit perspective.

**How to**. When you put the sacrifice bunt into effect, the batter merely **squares around** in bunting position and selects a pitch to bunt. For example, he may bunt a pitch foul and 'take' two called balls, giving him a 2-1 count, then successfully bunt the next pitch. He can try to bunt any pitch. However, on the hit-and-run and the steal, the runner 'goes on the pitch'. You, the manager, must select the pitch during the count on which you will try the play.

**Cost.** The sacrifice bunt, by definition, requires the batter to make an intentional out.[41] On the other hand, the hit-and-run and steal do not require you to intentionally give up an out. Of course, both plays may result in outs if poorly executed.

**Benefit.** A successful sacrifice bunt leaves a runner on second base. The successful hit-and-run will leave runners at first and third. The successful steal means that the runner advances one base.

---

41. The batter and the runner may both be safe on an attempted sacrifice bunt if it is a particularly well-placed bunt or a fielder makes an error.

**The skills of the players.** It is assumed that all players are able to bunt.[42] Stealing a base requires good speed and a 'good jump'. Getting a good jump, or 'going' at just the right moment, is a well-honed skill.

The hit-and-run requires a good contact hitter, or a batter who does not often swing-and-miss at pitches. The runner on a hit-and-run play should have at least average speed. If the batter misses the ball, the runner has to steal second base.

**When to use a 'play'.** The sacrifice bunt requires the batter to make an out in order to move a runner into scoring position so that two average or good hitters will have a chance to drive him in. For those reasons, the sacrifice bunt is almost always used with no outs except that, even with one out, a very weak hitter will be required to bunt.

The steal can be used with any number of outs.

The hit-and-run can be used with no outs or one out. A successful hit-and-run will usually leave runners on first and third base. A runner on third base with no outs or one out can score on a hit, on certain types of outs, or on a wild pitch. If the play was used with two outs, the runner on third base would need another hit (or wild pitch or balk) to score. No real advantage would be gained to justify the risk.

In the early innings, a manager traditionally uses these strategies in obvious situations or when the odds of success are strongly in his favor. He may decide not to use a strategy at all, even when he would have

42. Like most things that one assumes, it is not true. Not all players bunt well. Bunting merely involves sliding the top hand up the bat and cradling the bat gently (holding it horizontally over home plate), selecting a good pitch, and 'catching' the ball on the bat. It is an important fundamental skill that some players perform poorly.

a good chance of success. For example, a manager may decide not to use a hit-and-run with a man on first and no outs in the third inning even if he has a very good contact hitter at bat and a fast runner on first base. He has three outs to spend. Why not let the next three hitters bat? A double will usually score the runner and leave a runner on second base. Remember to consider what the other team would do — if you try the hit-and-run, the other team may use the pitchout on the pitch that you selected. Sometimes doing nothing or not using a strategy in the early innings is a good choice.

◆ ◆ ◆ ◆

By now you should have a feeling for how to use your players. You will always have to make some player substitutions, especially in the late innings. When choosing a relief pitcher or a pinch-hitter, you try to maintain the 'handedness' advantage, of course. The same handedness advantage goes to the pitcher. The opposite handedness advantage goes to the batter. The closer is a strike-out pitcher. Generally, the closer is used in the ninth inning when his team is ahead. Often the closer is brought into the game with runners on base. The best way to get out of a difficult situation, such as when the other team has runners on base, is to strike-out the batter.

Just a word on substitutions. Once a player is replaced by a substitute, the replaced player is out of the game and cannot return. The substitute player takes the spot of the replaced player in the batting order. Substitutions will be done in a simplified way in the hypothetical game that follows.

You did it! You are now fully qualified to manage a team at any level of baseball. Unfortunately, if a team plays poorly, another age-old baseball custom is to fire the manager (who usually has the least to do with it). Now, put your thinking cap on — you are the manager.

## The Eighth

# You Are The Manager

*If you do not recall the meaning of a term used in the next two chapters, please refer to the glossary.*

You decide to attend a Major League baseball game with your resident baseball expert or ResBex. Today, the TigerCats play the Otters in a critical late-season game.

You arrive at the ballpark on a bright, cool afternoon. A crisp breeze blows across the field. The grounds crew sprinkles the infield to settle the dust. The deep brown infield dirt sets off the rich green of the freshly mown grass. Vendors hawking hot dogs, beer, and peanuts shout above the low, busy rumble of the crowd. Every so often the faint, distinctive odor of cigar smoke wafts your way.

The managers have exchanged batting orders. The players finish warming up and trot in toward the bench.[43] The TigerCats are the home team. Therefore, the visiting Otters will bat first. Game time arrives.

The starting TigerCat players suddenly emerge from the dugout and trot out to their defensive positions on the field. The crowd responds to the TigerCats with a loud roar.

The TigerCats wear pristine white uniforms with 'TigerCats' emblazoned across the shirts in a bold orange script, edged with black piping.

43. The players' bench is located in the dugout. A dugout is just that. The design of dugouts varies, but most Major League dugouts are built a few feet below the level of the playing field (and some are level with the surface of the field).

93

The Otters' first and third base coaches take their positions in their respective coaching boxes.

Everyone stands at attention as the national anthem is played.

Then the umpire shouts: "Play Ball!"

As the first Otter batter walks to home plate you realize that you are in the TigerCat dugout. In fact, you are the TigerCat manager. "I must be dreaming," you think and are about to pinch yourself when a grizzled coach slaps you on the butt, spits, and utters a few garbled words of encouragement through a mouthful of chewing tobacco. You turn around to look into the crowd. Your ResBex is giving you the high sign. You swallow hard.

Recovering your sensibilities, you find a line-up card tucked in your back pocket. You do a quick study of both teams.

# The Line-Ups

Information on each team's players is listed on the line-up cards in a simplified way. First of all, do not be intimidated by all the numbers. When you are making strategy decisions, you will only be comparing the figures for two or three players. It is very easy.

Explanations of the symbols used follow.

## Batting Order

The symbols in the first column denote the player's position. C=Catcher, P=Pitcher, 1B=First baseman, 2B=Second baseman, SS=Shortstop, 3B=Third baseman, LF=left-fielder, CF=Center-fielder, RF=Right-fielder.

**'Bats'**: 'R' indicates that the player is a right-handed batter. 'L' indicates that the player is left-handed batter.

**Batting average**. Batting average is the percentage of at-bats in which a player gets a hit.

**Home runs**. The number of home runs gives you an estimate of the power-hitting ability of the batter.

**Strike-outs**. L, M, and H denote low, medium, and high. An H, for example, signifies that the batter strikes out a relatively high percentage of the time. Ordinarily, you would know the exact number of times that a batter struck out.

**Speed**. This column indicates the player's running speed. E = Excellent, VG = Very good, M = Medium, and S = Slow. A player with VG or E speed has the ability to steal bases.

## Substitute Position Players.

The non-starting position players listed here will be used as pinch hitters during the game. We shall assume that the pinch hitters just bat and then leave the game. Remember that a player is out of the game when another player pinch hits for him.

**Power**. With most Major League teams, the players in the starting line-up start just about every game the team plays (except the pitcher, of course).  Substitutes do not play often. Therefore, instead of stating the number of home runs that each has hit, which would be deceiving because of the low number of at-bats that a substitute gets, the L, M, and H are used to signify low, medium, and high power respectively.

## Available Pitchers.

Each team has a number of pitchers who are not available for the game. A starting pitcher is not available to pitch in relief because he is resting his arm for his next start. Some relief pitchers may have just pitched in the last few games and need time to rest. Only the available pitchers are listed. 'SR' signifies that a pitcher is a short-relief pitcher. 'C' signifies that he is the team's closer.

**ERA** means earned run average. The lower the ERA, the better the pitcher.

**Strike-outs.** Again, the L, M, and H designate low, medium, and high. The symbols are used to indicate how good a strike-out pitcher he is. For example, an H indicates that the pitcher strikes out a relatively high percentage of batters.

For purposes of this game, it is O.K. to use all your pinch-hitters or pitchers in nine innings. You may assume that the TigerCat-Otter game will not go into **extra innings.**

# OTTERS

| Batting Order | Bats | Batting Average | Home Runs | Strike-Outs | Speed |
|---|---|---|---|---|---|
| CF Baca | L | .340 | 1 | L | E |
| LF Lavelle | L | .295 | 0 | M | VG |
| 1B Waite | L | .308 | 11 | L | S |
| 3B Hernandez | R | .285 | 28 | H | S |
| RF McQuade | L | .225 | 21 | H | M |
| C Trenn | R | .245 | 10 | L | S |
| 2B Wilson | R | .240 | 0 | M | M |
| SS Smith | R | .238 | 0 | H | S |
| P Jones | R | .085 | 0 | H | S |

## Substitute position players

| | | | Power |
|---|---|---|---|
| Johnson | R | .235 | M |
| Peters | R | .220 | L |
| | | | |
| Anderson | L | .289 | H |
| Villalobos | L | .210 | L |

## Available pitchers

| | Throws | ERA | Strike Outs |
|---|---|---|---|
| CL Posie | R | 2.75 | H |
| SR Rose | R | 3.00 | M |
| | | | |
| SR Flowers | L | 3.50 | M |
| SR Gardenia | L | 4.00 | M |
| Starter - Jones | L | 3.10 | H |

# TIGERCATS

| Batting Order | Bats | Batting Average | Home Runs | Strike-Outs | Speed |
|---|---|---|---|---|---|
| CF Ford | R | .300 | 0 | L | VG |
| 2B Sanchez | R | .255 | 2 | L | M |
| LF Barnes | R | .310 | 15 | L | S |
| 1B Charles | L | .245 | 38 | H | S |
| RF Dodds | R | .275 | 18 | H | S |
| 3B Medrano | R | .270 | 7 | M | S |
| SS Enright | R | .263 | 0 | M | M |
| C  Handy | R | .233 | 10 | H | S |
| P  Inkster | R | .100 | 0 | H | S |

## Substitute position players

| | | | Power |
|---|---|---|---|
| Becker | R | .245 | M |
| Thomas | R | .238 | L |
| | | | |
| Nieves | L | .290 | L |
| O'Leary | L | .240 | L |

## Available pitchers

| | Throws | ERA | Strike Outs |
|---|---|---|---|
| CL  Green | R | 1.60 | H |
| SR  Rojas | R | 3.30 | M |
| | | | |
| SR  White | L | 2.80 | H |
| SR  Black | L | 3.50 | L |
| (Starter - Inkster) | R | 3.75 | L |

## The First Inning

Your starting pitcher is Inkster, a right-hander. You recall reading that Inkster is an aging, but savvy pitcher whose best pitch is the curveball. He has a good change-up. His fastball is below average. Inkster's 'earned run average' is 3.75, somewhat higher (or worse) than average. The Otters' pitcher is 'Smokin' Joe Jones. He throws left-handed. Smokin' Joe has a great fastball and an excellent slider. His other pitch is a change-up. Smokin' Joe averages about one strike-out an inning, a very high rate. Jones' ERA of 3.10 is quite good. Your pitcher doesn't strike out many batters.

You examine the Otters' batting order.

You note the batting averages of the players. Baca, the 'lead off' hitter, has one of the highest averages in the league. In fact, the first four Otter batters have high averages but then there is a dropoff. The other batters are below average hitters.

Baca is a superior base-stealer. Lavelle is also fast.

The left-handed Baca will have the 'handedness' advantage against right-handed TigerCat pitcher, Inkster. The second and third batters, Lavelle and Waite are also left-handed. Both are excellent hitters. You note from the home run statistics that Hernandez and McQuade, the fourth and fifth hitters, are good power hitters while Waite and Trenn also have some power.

You glance at the rest of the players, noting the non-starting position players who may be used as pinch hitters later in the game and the Otters' relief pitchers.

You are particularly concerned about the 'top of the order', the first few Otter hitters, because all have high batting averages and also have the handedness advantage against Inkster. If any of them get on base, then 'clean up hitter' Hernandez, and possibly McQuade, will have a chance to drive them in.

The Otters' lead off batter, Baca, steps up to the plate.

"Now, let's see," you think. "The batter has the handedness advantage. Baca will hit pitches over the middle or inside of the plate hardest. Inkster does not have a good fastball. A good fastball can be thrown anywhere except down the middle, so Inkster has to hit the 'outside corner' with his curveball." Your baseball knowledge is beginning to come to you. "He will throw the fastball only when he needs to 'change speeds' or if he has to throw a strike when he is 'behind in the count'. He may also change speeds by throwing the change-up. Above all, he should try to get ahead of the batter on the count. We certainly do not want to walk the lead-off batter, especially a fast runner like Baca. . ."

Inkster's first pitch is a curveball on the 'outside corner'. Baca 'takes' it. It is called a strike.

His second pitch is another curveball. Baca swings and hits a hard line drive that lands outside the first base foul line, a foul ball. The count is 0-2.

On his third pitch, Inkster uses his mediocre fastball to 'brush back' Baca. Baca stumbles backward awkwardly, barely evading being hit by the pitch.

Baca glares at veteran pitcher Inkster who maintains an unperturbed, businesslike expression. Clearly, the pitch ruffled the Otter's feathers.

"If Inkster can throw a pitch on the outside corner, he is going to get this guy out," the coach says to you.

"Right, Zack," you say as your coach's name suddenly comes to you somehow. The brushback pitch puts a jolt of fear in the batter. It elicits primitive self-preservation instincts that make the batter more hesitant to stride strongly into the next pitch. The brushback is almost always followed by a pitch over the outside corner.

Inkster's next pitch is a knee high change-up on the outside corner.

Baca, the timing of his swing having been disrupted by the brushback and the change of speeds, has a weak swing at the ball. He sends an easy ground ball to second baseman Sanchez. Sanchez fields the ball and throws to first baseman Charles who catches the ball while positioned with one foot on first base. The throw arrives before Baca and he is called out by the umpire.

The fans applaud appreciatively.

Lavelle, the next batter, hits a line drive that lands in center field. Center fielder Ford fields the ball and throws into second base. Lavelle holds at first base with a single.

Lavelle, who has better than average speed, leads off first base. Inkster assumes the 'set', or 'stretch', position. Inkster tries a 'pickoff throw'. Lavelle gets back to first base before Charles can tag him with the ball. He is safe.

"Inkster has got to 'hold the runner close' to first base," you think, "because Lavelle is fast. He may attempt to steal second base. Inkster will try to keep the runner close. Inkster does not want him to get a 'good jump', or good start toward second, especially if he is stealing." Your baseball mind has slipped into gear.

Inkster again assumes the stretch position. He spins and throws to first. The play is very close, but Lavelle gets back safely.

Inkster throws a curveball to the left-handed hitting Waite. Waite hits a hard ground ball right at second baseman Sanchez. Sanchez flips the ball to shortstop Enright who steps on second base well before the sliding Lavelle arrives. Enright then throws to first base.

First baseman Charles catches the ball before the slow-footed Waite arrives. Lavelle and Waite are out. Double play! The inning is over.

The TigerCat fans cheer the snappy double play as the TigerCats trot off the field. You admire the performance of the veteran Inkster who kept the Otters literally off-balance by using the brushback pitch (followed by a pitch over the outside corner), holding the runner close at first base and mixing up his pitches well. He is using all the tricks of a veteran pitcher.

You now study the TigerCats batting order. You note that Ford and Barnes have the highest batting averages. Barnes, Charles, and Dodds have good power, but the TigerCats do not have much speed. Ford is the only base stealing threat. The Otters' pitcher, Jones, is left-handed. The first three TigerCat batters are right-handed batters and will have the handedness advantage against Jones. However, this advantage is somewhat diminished because Jones throws mainly fastballs and sliders. These are pitches that can be effectively thrown anywhere in the strike zone (except down the middle), unlike the curveball, which is generally effective only when thrown on the outside part of the plate.

Tigercats Ford and Sanchez flied out. Barnes hit a home run over the left field wall and received a long ovation. Charles struck out.

Neither team scored in the second inning.

# The Third Inning

The Otters failed to score in the top of the third inning. The game moves to the bottom of the third inning. The TigerCats, still leading 1-0, are at bat.

Handy leads off. He walks.

"What are you gonna do?" the grizzled coach mumbles and spits.

"Huh?" you say.

Your baseball mind kicks back into gear. "Let's see," you think, considering your options, "Steal, sacrifice bunt, or hit-and-run." You calmly analyze the factors to be considered.

Pitcher Inkster is the next batter. He is a very poor hitter as are almost all pitchers. Handy is very slow (as are almost all catchers).

"It's early in the game, should I try to get Handy into 'scoring position'?" you think.

**What would you do...?**

Should you attempt...

A. A steal?

B. A sacrifice bunt?

C. A hit-and-run?

D. Do nothing?

◆ ◆ ◆ ◆

## Answer

A. The attempted steal. Handy is slow. He has virtually no chance to steal second base successfully.

B.    The sacrifice bunt.  Handy needs help getting to second base. Inkster is a poor hitter.  Should Inkster give up his chance to get a hit in order to get the runner into 'scoring position'?

Absolutely.

C.    The hit-and-run. The hit-and-run is a poor choice because Inkster is a poor 'contact' hitter and Handy is slow.  If Inkster misses the ball, Handy will be thrown out at second base.

It is important to have a good 'contact' hitter at bat on the hit-and-run.  When the play is on, the batter must swing at the pitch.  If he misses the pitch, the runner, who is off and running, must steal second base.

Inkster is a poor hitter who strikes out frequently and Handy is slow. If Inkster misses the pitch, a likelihood, Handy will almost certainly be thrown out at second base.  The hit-and-run would be a bad choice.

D.    Do nothing. Doing nothing would mean that you would allow Inkster to bat.  Inkster's chances of getting a hit are small.  His batting average is .100.  Also, he and Handy are slow, increasing the risk that Inkster may ground into a double play.  Playing by the book dictates that the pitcher be allowed to try to get a hit only when you have no other choice.  For example, the pitcher is allowed to bat when he is the lead-off batter in an inning, when no one is on base when he is at bat, or when there are two outs.

The sacrifice bunt is clearly the correct choice.

Give yourself +1 if you selected B, the sacrifice bunt.

Give yourself -1 if you selected A, C, or D.

◆ ◆ ◆ ◆

The Otters also think that you will attempt the sacrifice bunt. Their third baseman is 'playing in' on the grass. When Inkster 'squares around', to bunt, the third baseman charges a few steps toward the plate. The first baseman, who was 'holding the runner on', also charges in on the pitch.

Inkster bunts. It is a good bunt, rolling weakly between the pitcher and the third baseman. The Otter third baseman throws Inkster out at first base (the second baseman covering). Handy, who had a good lead, advances to second base.

Now, there is one out and a man on second. Ford, the next batter, hit a fly ball to left field. Handy went 'halfway', but returned to second base when the ball was caught. As a practical matter, a runner on second base does not have a chance to tag up and advance on a fly ball to left field because the left fielder has a short throw to third base.

Sanchez hits a hard ground ball 'up the middle'. The ball rolls into center field where it is fielded by Baca. The slow-footed Handy begins running toward third base. The ball is behind him. As he approaches third base Handy looks at his third base coach for guidance. The third base coach is windmilling his arms frantically, signalling Handy to score. Center fielder Baca throws toward the 'cut off man', the Otter first baseman, who is positioned between the pitcher's mound and home plate. The cut off man catches the throw instead of letting it go through to the catcher. Handy scores. Because the throw was cut off, Sanchez had to stop at first base with a single.

Barnes 'popped out' to end the inning. The TigerCats lead 2-0.

John W. Hood

# The Fourth Inning

In the top of the fourth inning, Otter Waite hit a ball that rolled into the 'gap' in right-center field. He advanced to second base with a double.

On a 1-0 count, Hernandez successfully 'hit behind the runner'. He grounded out to second, while Waite advanced to third base.

Inkster's first pitch to McQuade bounced off home plate. TigerCat catcher Handy was unable to block it. Waite scored on the 'wild pitch.'

Then McQuade doubled.

Trenn singled, driving in McQuade.

With one out, Wilson hit a high-bouncing ground ball to third. TigerCat third baseman Medrano got a force out at second base on Trenn. Trenn slid into second baseman Sanchez in order to 'break up the double play'. As a result, Sanchez was unable to throw to first base for the attempted double play. Wilson was safe at first base on a 'fielder's choice'.

Wilson was then picked off first base by Inkster on a call that was disputed by the Otters. Wilson protested vehemently to the umpire. The Otters' manager ran out on the field to continue the argument. He complained that Inkster had 'balked'. The umpire did not agree and, eventually, the hot Otters returned to the dugout.

The TigerCats failed to score in the bottom of the fourth.

# The Fifth Inning

In the top of the fifth inning the score is 2-2. Smith leads off for the Otters. He grounds out to first baseman Charles. Jones strikes out. Baca singles.

There are two outs and a 'man on first'. **What do you think the Otters are going to do?**

A.  Attempt to steal second base?

B.  Try the hit-and-run play?

C.  Try a sacrifice bunt?

D.  Do nothing?

## Answer

A.  The attempted steal. The Otters' Baca is a superior base stealer. If he steals second base, he will be in scoring position. Lavelle, the next batter, is a very good hitter.

B.  The hit-and-run. There are two outs. A successful hit-and-run would leave runners on first and third base. Unless Inkster throws a wild pitch (or a balk is called) or the Cats commit an error, the Otters would need yet another hit to score a run. The hit-and-run is not used with two outs.

C.  The sacrifice bunt. The sacrifice bunt is out of the question since the sacrifice bunt involves making an intentional out — the third out of the inning.

D.  Do nothing. Remember that, in the early innings, doing nothing is often a good choice. Lavelle is a good hitter (a .295 average) and a double would score Baca. Or, if Lavelle gets on base (hit, walk, hit-by-pitch, error), then Waite, an excellent hitter (a .308 average) with good power, would bat. He is paid to drive in runs. Baca may be thrown out on an attempted steal.

The most important factors in this situation are the base stealing ability of Baca and the fact that there are two outs. The book says to try the steal. 'Do nothing' is a close second.

Give yourself +1 if you said 'steal' or 'do nothing'. Give yourself -1 if you said sacrifice bunt or hit-and-run.

◆ ◆ ◆ ◆

Baca did steal second base. Lavelle hit a ground ball that Sanchez muffed badly. It was called an error. Lavelle advanced to first and Baca to third. Waite walked to load the bases.

Fortunately, power-hitter Hernandez flied out to center fielder Wilson to end the inning.

You breathed a sigh of relief. The Otters could have scored a few runs in the fifth inning. Although the players were responsible for the problems — stolen base, error, walk — the manager is always held accountable for lost games as part of baseball tradition.

◆ ◆ ◆ ◆

In the bottom of the fifth inning, the score is still tied 2-2. Ford leads off for the TigerCats.

Ford singles sharply to left field.

You feel Zack's gaze.

Again, you analyze the situation. Tie score, no outs, man on first. Sanchez is now at bat.

Zack cannot contain himself any longer. "What are you gonna do?", he asks.

**What would you do...**

Would you attempt a...

A.  Steal?

B.  Sacrifice bunt?

C.  Hit-and-run?

D.    Do nothing?

## Answer

A.    The steal.  Ford has better than average speed but he may be thrown out at second base.  Remember to always look ahead a couple of batters when considering a strategy. You have your best batters coming to bat this inning.  Your third, fourth, and fifth batters have good power.  Ford would score from first base on a double.  It is still early in a tie game.  You want to give the hitters a chance to drive him in and possibly have a 'big inning'.  The attempted steal is a somewhat risky option.

B.    The sacrifice bunt.  Do you want Sanchez to make an out in order to get Ford into scoring position?  Sanchez is only an average hitter.  Your best batter, Barnes, is batting next.  Then your best power hitter, Charles, is next.[44]  The sacrifice bunt is not a bad choice either. Bearing in mind that it is early in a tie game, you must decide whether you want to intentionally give up an out.

C.    The hit-and-run.  The essential elements for a hit-and-run are in place.  The batter is a good contact hitter and the runner is fast.  Even if the batter swings and misses, the runner has a good chance to steal second base.  A successful hit-and-run would leave runners on first and third base with no outs.  The TigerCats would be in position for a 'big inning'.  A runner on third base with less than two outs could score on

---

44. If you sacrificed successfully, the Otters would not intentionally walk Charles, who is an excellent hitter.  The intentional walk is generally used as a late inning strategy when the potential run scored by the intentionally walked batter would be meaningless.  Here, Charles' run would not be meaningless.

a hit or certain types of outs. If the hit-and-run worked, you would have an excellent chance to score at least one run, if not more.

D.   Do nothing. Doing nothing, or not putting any plays on, is often an underrated choice. Sometimes a manager will do nothing even when the elements favoring success of some offensive 'play' are in place. The hit-and-run play appears to be a good risk. But a double would also score Ford from first base. There are no outs. The game is only in the fifth inning. The next batters, Sanchez and Barnes, have the opposite handedness advantage against Jones. Why not just let the hitters hit? An unsuccessful steal or even a successful sacrifice bunt will cost you one out. An unsuccessful hit-and-run may cost you an out (or two). An out means that one additional batter will not get a chance to bat.

There is not always a clearly 'correct' choice of strategy. You do not want to 'overmanage'.

'Do nothing' is a good choice too.

Give yourself +1 for choices C, the hit-and-run, or D, do nothing. Do not deduct any points for choices A or B.

**How will the defensive team defend the possible hit-and-run play?**

**Answer**

The pitchout.

A pitchout is a fastball thrown about a foot-and-half outside the plate. The catcher jumps out to catch the ball. The pitchout is a particularly good defense against the hit-and-run because the batter cannot reach the pitch with his bat. It is also much easier to throw out the runner on a pitchout because the catcher receives the ball quickly and while he is standing in throwing position. Of course, the pitchout will be called a ball.

A second, more subtle way for the pitcher to defend against the hit-and-run, is to throw a difficult pitch for the batter to hit to the fielder's vacated position. Right-handed batter Sanchez has to hit the ball to the right side of the infield. A pitch thrown high and inside, even if thrown for a strike, is the hardest type of strike for him to hit to the right side. The pitcher may also throw a pitch well outside, that the batter cannot reach with his bat. It would be called a ball, of course.

Give yourself +1 if you guessed the pitchout or high and inside strike or outside pitch. Do not deduct any points if you didn't think of these defenses.

◆ ◆ ◆ ◆

You are mulling over whether or not to use the hit-and-run. "I must decide the best pitch during the count on which to call the hit-and-run play, if I use it at all," you think. "The Otters may use the pitchout or give the batter a difficult pitch to hit to the right side of the infield. It would be to my advantage to use the play when the batter is ahead in the count because then the pitcher has to throw a strike."

Back in the dugout, Zack is insistent, "What are you gonna do?"

"I'm going to use the hit-and-run if Sanchez gets ahead in the count," you say. Sanchez is an average hitter but he has the opposite-handedness advantage against the pitcher. He may get a good pitch to hit (in his 'pull zone'). And if it is a ball, Sanchez will have the count in his favor.

"Holy Cow, I'm talking baseball," you think.

In fact, the first pitch is a fastball that is several inches outside. It is called a ball.

Zack looks at you.

"Not yet," you say to him. "Let Sanchez swing at the next pitch if it is good. The count is in his favor." The second pitch is an inside fastball but it is too far inside and is called a ball by the umpire.

Now you put the hit-and-run play on, figuring that the Otters will not pitchout because they do not want to have a 3-0 count on Sanchez. The pitcher needs to throw a strike.

Ford goes on the pitch and Otter second baseman Lavelle runs over to cover the base. Jones' pitch is a slider over the inner third of the plate. Although it is a difficult pitch to hit to the right side of the infield, Sanchez hits it off the bat handle. The ball rolls through the area that Lavelle vacated and into right field.

Ford easily advances to third base. Sanchez is credited with a single. The hit-and-run was perfectly executed by Sanchez, a skillful contact hitter.

With runners on first and third base and no outs, Barnes hit a hard line drive caught by third baseman Hernandez. The runners, waiting for the ball to 'go through', got back to their bases safely.

Then, Charles sent a long fly ball into deep right field. Ford, the runner on third base, tagged up. Otter right-fielder McQuade caught the ball but saw that he would have no chance to throw out Ford at the plate. Ford scored on the sacrifice fly. McQuade threw the ball to second base. As a result, Sanchez had to hold at first base.

With two outs and a man on first, Dodds struck out, but the TigerCats lead 3-2.

Unfortunately, the Otters scored one run in the sixth inning. The game was tied the game 3-3 after six innings.

# The Late Innings

## The Seventh Inning

Old Inkster was doing a masterful job of mixing his pitches.

The seventh inning begins the 'late innings', the end-game stage. Early in the game, the teams simply try to score as many runs as they can. Limited, high-percentage strategy is used in the early innings because most strategy involves either giving up an out or risking a base runner. In the seventh inning managers begin using more strategy and making personnel changes such as substituting relief pitchers and pinch hitters. The team that is behind will use a pinch hitter in the place of the pitcher and the weaker hitters. Both teams will bring in relief pitchers to get the handedness advantage against the batter. Sometimes that pitcher pitches to just one batter, then another pitcher is brought in. In the late innings of a close game managers use strategy to attempt to score one run.

Baca, the lead-off batter for the Otters in the seventh, hit a hard line drive that landed in foul territory.

Inkster's next two pitches were called balls.

Inkster is clearly struggling.

"Inkster has thrown a lot of pitches. He looks tired. He could be running out of gas," you think. "With the score tied, each batter is important now." You decide to bring in a relief pitcher, but the reliever needs time to warm up.

You turn to Zack. "Zack, call time-out and go kill some time with Inkster. Take as much time as the umpire will allow."

The umpire raises both arms above his head to signal that time is out.

The TigerCat infielders gather around the mound as Zack walks to the mound with the reluctant gait of a child whose parent has just said to him: "Come here so I can spank you." His lackadaisical walk is intentional, of course. He is trying to buy a little time for the relief pitcher to warm up.

Zack arrives at this critical juncture to find Inkster, Charles, and Sanchez discussing where to play golf after the game. Zack tells Inkster, "This is the last batter that you are going to pitch to."

As Zack began the walk to the mound, you had a relief pitcher begin to warm up. Now, he has spent about a minute or so on the mound. The home plate umpire, who was standing behind home plate since the time-out was called, begins walking to the mound.

Traditionally the umpire allows the team a couple minutes for a time-out. When the umpire reaches the mound, the time-out is over.

Zack claps his hands, utters a few words of encouragement to the players, and trots back to the dugout.

Inkster missed with a curveball. The count is 3-1. On the 3-1 pitch, Inkster, needing a strike, cranked up his tired, old fastball. Baca hit a long drive into the right-center field 'gap'. The ball rolled all the way to the wall. Baca stopped at second base with a double.

The go-ahead run is now in scoring position.

Left-handed batter Lavelle waits in the batter's box.

Your relief pitcher is warmed up. You call time-out and walk to the mound yourself. Traditionally, the manager removes the pitcher himself.

Just before you arrive at the mound, you signal for your relief pitcher to come into the game. You congratulate Inkster on pitching well. Inkster gives you the ball and trots into the dugout to the appreciative applause of the TigerCat faithful.

Remember to cross out Inkster's name on your line-up card. Assume that all of your relief pitchers are warmed up. **Which relief pitcher would you bring into the game?**

A. White?

B. Black?

C. Green?

D. Rojas?

Hint: Look at who is scheduled to bat for the Otters.

### Answer

In order to have the same-handedness advantage, you want a left-handed pitcher to pitch to the Otters' left-handed batters. Lavelle and Waite are left-handed. Since they are excellent hitters, the Otters will not use pinch hitters for them.

Green and Rojas are right-handed pitchers. And Green is your 'closer'. The closer usually comes into the game in the eighth or ninth inning when his team is ahead (and, much less frequently, when it is tied). Using a right-handed pitcher would not be wise.

Your left-handers are White and Black. White has a better 'earned run average' than Black. White also is a very good strike-out pitcher while

Black is not. There is no better way to get out of a difficult situation than to get a strike-out. The better choice would be White.

Give yourself +1 for choosing White, -1 for choosing Green or Rojas, and do not add or deduct any points for choosing Black.

◆ ◆ ◆ ◆

You give White the ball and make sure that he is aware of the situation. "Runner on second, no outs," you tell him.

Lavelle hit the ball sharply, grounding it to second baseman Sanchez's left. Sanchez fielded the ball and threw out Lavelle at first base while runner Baca advanced to third base. By pulling the ball, left-handed Lavelle successfully moved the runner.

Of course, you well know that a runner on third base with less than two outs can score on a hit, error, various types of outs or a wild pitch.

Waite walked.

Then, with runners on first and third base and one out, power-hitter Hernandez struck out. McQuade flied out to end the inning.

Zack winked and the TigerCat faithful breathed a sigh of relief.

In the bottom of the seventh inning, the TigerCats scored one run on Barnes' second home run of the game.

The TigerCats took a 4-3 lead into the eighth inning.

## The Eighth Inning

Thinking ahead as the TigerCats batted in the seventh, you had another relief pitcher warm up. Trenn, Wilson, and Smith are due to bat for the Otters. You bring in your new relief pitcher.

## Who would you select...?

A.  Green?

B.  Rojas?

C.  Black?

## Answer

The next three Otter batters are right-handed, making this an easy choice.

(C)  Black is left-handed.

(A)  Green is the closer.  Too early.

(B)  Rojas, a right-handed short relief pitcher, is the best choice.

Give yourself +1 for choosing Rojas.  Give yourself -1 for choosing Black.  Do not add or deduct any points for choosing Green.

Rojas is brought into the game to replace White.  (Cross off White's name.)

Trenn singled.  Wilson put down a sacrifice bunt, moving Trenn to second base.

Again, you are thinking ahead.  "The sacrifice bunt," you think, "means that the Otters will give two fair or good hitters a chance to drive in the runner and tie the game.  Therefore, they will be using a pinch hitter for the pitcher.  Of course, they will select a left-handed pinch hitter."

You have your last available left-handed pitcher, Black, warm up so that he will be ready to pitch to the pinch hitter.

Right-handed batter Smith flied out to center field. Trenn remained at second base.

With two outs and a man on second, the Otters' pitcher Jones is due to bat. As expected, the Otters send up their best left-handed pinch hitter, Anderson. (Cross off Jones' name.)

You counter by bringing in left-handed relief pitcher Black.[45](Cross off Rojas' name.)

Black hit Anderson with a pitch. Anderson was awarded first base automatically. Now there are runners on first and second with two outs.

Black stayed in the game to pitch to Baca, who is also left-handed. Since Baca is the Otter's best hitter, they do not use a pinch hitter merely to gain the handedness advantage.

Baca hit a line drive that was caught by Sanchez, ending the inning. You breathe yet another sigh of relief.

In the bottom of the eighth inning, the TigerCats lead 4-3. They have three right-handed batters due to bat. Since the Otters used a pinch-hitter to bat for their pitcher, Jones, he was out of the game. The Otters bring in right-handed relief pitcher Rose (who will fill the ninth spot in the batting order).

45. You may be wondering "Who goes first — the manager who puts in the pinch hitter or the manager who puts in the relief pitcher?" The team at bat must always have a player scheduled to bat and a pitcher who enters a game must pitch to at least one batter. A better question is "Who goes last?" The answer: the team at bat. Once the batting team sees which reliever will pitch they select a pinch hitter.

Dodds thrills the crowd with a long fly ball that Otter left fielder Wilson catches with his back against the wall. Medrano hits a routine ground ball to short. He is thrown out at first.

With two outs, Enright hits a line drive in the gap in left-center field. He stops at second with a double.

The crowd cheers enthusiastically.

Handy, who has a poor batting average, but some power, is due to bat next.

Zack, chewing busily, spits and turns to you.

**What would you do. . .?**

◆ ◆ ◆ ◆

### Answer

Play for one run in the late innings.

If Enright scores, the TigerCats will take a two run lead into the ninth inning. Such a lead would be very hard for the Otters to overcome. Enright has average speed but a single (into the outfield) will probably drive him in.

Your best chance to get a single would be to use pinch-hitter Nieves, who has a batting average of .290, compared to Handy's batting average of .233. The fact that Handy can hit with power is less important when a single will drive in the critical run. Also, Otter pitcher Rose would have the same-handedness advantage against right-hander Handy. Then left-handed batter Nieves will have the handedness advantage against the Otter pitcher, right? (Trick question.)

No. Remember that when you are considering strategy, step two is to consider what the other team will do. The Otters will bring in a left-handed pitcher if you send Nieves up to bat. However, Nieves is a better choice of batter than Handy because the book says to always play to your strengths. You want your better hitter at the plate.[46]

Give yourself +1 for choosing Nieves to pinch hit. Give yourself -1 if you let Handy bat or chose another strategy. Do not deduct any points if you chose another pinch hitter because all the TigerCat pinch hitters have better batting averages than Handy.

With two outs and a runner on second, Nieves steps to the plate. Left-handed pitcher Flowers replaces Rose for the Otters. (Cross off Rose's name.)

Nieves grounds out to second to the groans of the TigerCat fans.

We will assume that Nieves is a catcher and stays in the game, replacing Handy. Cross off Handy's name.

## The Ninth Inning

The score is 4-3 in favor of the TigerCats as the top of the ninth inning begins. You leave your left-handed relief pitcher, Black, in the game because the Otters' first two batters are left-handed.

46. Would you rather have Handy bat against Rose or would you prefer to have Nieves bat against Flowers (the pitcher that the Otters will bring into the game if you pinch hit Nieves)? The team at bat gets to make the last move. You just need a single. Nieves (.290) is a better hitter than Handy (.233) and Flowers (3.50) is not as good a pitcher as Rose (3.00). The match-up of Nieves versus Flowers matches your better hitter against their lesser pitcher. Very clever move.

Left-handed batter Lavelle leads off for the Otters. Lavelle flies out to center field. Waite singles.

You sense the restlessness of the crowd as power hitter Hernandez steps to the plate with one out and a man on first.

Zack looks your way again.

**What would you do?**

◆ ◆ ◆ ◆

## Answer

Bring in the closer! The closer's most frequent role is to come into the game during the ninth inning when his team is ahead. Your closer, Green, is right-handed. He is an excellent strike-out pitcher with an excellent earned run average. You need a strike-out. Hernandez and McQuade, the next two Otters scheduled to bat, strike-out frequently. The closer is paid to finish games. He is frequently brought into the game just to get the last out or two.

If you said 'the closer', give yourself +1. Do not deduct any points for another answer.

◆ ◆ ◆ ◆

(Cross off Black.)

Closer Green's first pitch is a high fast ball in the strike zone. Hernandez is apparently expecting a fastball because he smacks it down the left field line for a double.

Waite scores.

"(Bleep!)", Zack blurts out.

The air was out of the balloon. Fans were still as the hated Otters tied the game.

And the Otters still have a runner in scoring position with one out. McQuade strikes out.

Trenn grounds out to third to end the inning.

Recall that 'earned run average' is a statistic that states how many runs a pitcher gives up per game (that are not the result of an error).

**Who is charged with the run that the Otters scored?**

### Answer

Black. The pitcher who allowed a batter or batters to get on base is charged with any runs that the players score. Black allowed Waite to get on base (single). He is charged with the run even though Waite scored when Green was pitching.

Give yourself +1 for a correct answer. Make no deduction for an incorrect answer.

In the bottom of the ninth inning, the game is tied 4-4.

As the dejected TigerCats trot back into the dugout to take their turn at bat, the organist begins to play familiar chords. You hear strident, high-pitched voices of youngsters chanting, "Let's go Cats! Let's go Cats! . . ."

Because this is an important game, the Otters elect to bring in their closer, Posie, who is right-handed.

The pitcher, Green, is due to bat for the TigerCats. Naturally, you will use a pinch-hitter. You select your remaining left-handed pinch-hitter, O'Leary. (Cross off Green.)

O'Leary is one of the TigerCats' more colorful players. A fan favorite, he is a fiery journeyman player. Because of his fondness for the night life, he has a history of missing the team bus. One day, as the bus pulled away sans O'Leary, a teammate commented, "O'Leary swings and misses, again." The unfortunate nickname, "Misses", stuck.

The Otter closer, Posie, is a very large man with a sinister-looking Fu Manchu moustache. He is known for his great fastball, ability to throw strikes, and methods of intimidation.

O'Leary stepped into the batters' box. The count quickly went to 0-2. Posie was overpowering him with fastballs and sliders. It stayed at 0-2 as O'Leary was able to foul off a series of fastballs and sliders.

The fans sat quietly. O'Leary seemed no match for the power pitcher.

O'Leary pawed at the dirt in the batter's box with his back foot, digging a foothold. This behavior apparently upset Posie, because the next pitch sent O'Leary sprawling backwards into the dirt.

The fans lustily booed Posie.

"I guess that's Posie's way of telling O'Leary not to get too, too comfortable in the batter's box," you say knowledgeably.

"Mgumph," said Zack, nodding and chewing.

O'Leary got up and dusted himself off. With a threatening scowl, he slowly raised his bat and pointed it purposefully at Posie.

The memorable gesture stirred up the fans. The crowd suddenly came to life, clapping, stomping, and cheering O'Leary noisily.

The next pitch, as expected, was a fastball aimed at the outside corner. Fortunately, it was called a ball because, for all his bluster, O'Leary's legs were still a bit rubbery.

On the 2-2 pitch, O'Leary stroked a clean single up the middle.

The crowd reacted wildly.

O'Leary has slightly better than average speed. Now, Ford, a .300 hitter, is at bat. O'Leary represents the winning run.

You briefly consider the sacrifice bunt but decide not to 'take the bat out of the hands' of Ford, an excellent hitter. Ford singled into right field and O'Leary was able to advance to third base. You are startled by the sudden explosion from the crowd.

Now, there are no outs and men on first and third base.

An Otters coach called time and trotted out of the dugout. The coach and the infielders form a ring around Posie to discuss strategy.

As Sanchez steps into the batter's box you notice that the Otters, are 'playing the infield in'. Playing the infield in gives them the opportunity to throw O'Leary out at home plate on a ground ball. The outfielders are also playing shallow.

The fans are on their feet!

You consider your next move. A long fly ball or a ground ball through the drawn in infield will win the game. You briefly consider the squeeze play. Since the infield is playing in, you reject the safety squeeze because the infielders would get to the bunt quickly.

You consider the suicide squeeze. "If I use the suicide squeeze," you think, "Sanchez would probably get a good pitch to bunt because Posie throws a lot of strikes. While the play may succeed, Sanchez would also drive in the run with a ground ball that is not hit right at an infielder or with a moderately long fly ball. Sanchez is a good contact hitter. An unsuccessful suicide squeeze would be disastrous because the runner on third, the potential winning run, would be out."

You decide to let Sanchez bat. The fans groan as he pops out. The runners remain on their bases.

With one out, your best hitter, Barnes, steps to the plate.

He is warmly greeted by TigerCats fans. And by the Otters. They give him an intentional walk to load the bases with one out.

The Otters walked Barnes for two reasons. First, the Otters were not going to let the TigerCats best hitter beat them. The Otters would rather pitch to Charles, who has a batting average of .245, than Barnes, who is batting .310, when just a single will win the game. The only runner that the Otters are concerned with is O'Leary, who is standing on third base. If he scores, the Otters lose. No other runner matters. Therefore, the Otters do not have to pitch to the TigerCats best hitter. Secondly, walking Barnes loads the bases, creating a force at every base. The Otters could get a force out at home plate or a double play on a ground ball. Walking Barnes creates more opportunities to get outs.

Why didn't the Otters walk Sanchez to create a force at every base? Because they would have had to pitch to Barnes. Sanchez is a weaker hitter. In other words, the Otters took a chance on getting Sanchez out without the run scoring (with no outs and runners on first and third) so that they would not have to pitch to Barnes (with no outs and the bases loaded). Now, with one out, a double play will end the inning and Charles is slow.

A secondary consideration in the Otters' decision to walk Barnes is that Charles and Dodds, who are due to bat next, both strike-out frequently. Closer Posie is paid to strike-out batters. In their conference on the mound, the Otters obviously decided to pitch to Sanchez and walk Barnes.

With the bases loaded and one out, the count went to 3-1 on Charles. The fans noisily cheered each called ball.

"We need a sacrifice fly," Zack says.

On the 3-1 pitch, Charles guesses that Posie will throw a fastball. If Posie throws a ball, he walks in the winning run.

The fans are on their feet. The pitch is a fastball. Charles swings mightily, hitting a very high fly ball to medium-deep right field. Otter right-fielder McQuade, who had been playing shallow, backs up a few steps to wait under the fly ball. McQuade has the strongest throwing arm on the team.

O'Leary retreats to third base to tag up, standing in a crouch at third base.

McQuade catches the ball.

O'Leary takes off for home as McQuade uncorks a powerful throw.

O'Leary slides into home plate under the diving catcher.

"SAFE!"

The crowd explodes! The TigerCats won!

Zack grips your hand firmly.

The next day, photos of the action appeared on the sports pages. Perhaps the most memorable was that of O'Leary, standing at home plate, scowling and pointing at Posie after he had been brushed back. The caption read **"Misses' O'Leary's scowl ignites city."**

The TigerCats went on to win the championship that year. The fans talked for years about the pivotal TigerCat-Otter game that you had managed.

# Conclusion

Congratulations! You understand baseball. These final 'test' chapters incorporate the fundamentals and all of the important strategies that were discussed in the book. In fact, you learned much more than you need to know in order to simply understand what is happening in a baseball game. That was intentional. Most fans prefer to passively watch the game, not actively 'manage' the team. They do second-guess the manager periodically though. But knowing 'inside baseball', or what the players and managers are trying to do, gives you an enriched understanding of baseball.

Before you read this book, you may have thought that a pitcher just throws the ball as hard as he can and the batter takes a good hard swing at it. In Little League baseball, that is pretty much true. Strategy becomes a little more sophisticated at each higher level of baseball. But baseball remains a simple game. Every strategy consideration ultimately depends upon the ability of the pitcher to pitch and the ability of the hitter to hit.

Baseball strategy (like the same and opposite handedness advantage) will become second nature to you soon. Particularly if you have a ResBex to watch games with you. Every true ResBex loves to impart baseball wisdom and tell anecdotes. After watching a few games and discussing plays with your ResBex you will understand more subtleties.

For example, it was repeatedly stressed that the closer's most frequent role is to pitch in the ninth inning when his team is ahead. But, it was also stated that the closer sometimes pitches in the eighth inning. Why wouldn't a team bring in the closer in the eighth inning in a situation when it really needs a strike-out? It might. But the closer may be scheduled to bat in the ninth inning. The team would either have to pinch-hit for him — removing him from the game (he could not pitch the ninth inning) — or let him bat. They are equally bad choices.

With that, I also close.[47]

47. This book is not intended to be an absolutely complete explanation of all rules and strategies. For example, a batter is sometimes allowed to attempt to advance after 'striking out'. What? If the umpire calls a pitch (that a batter takes) strike three or if the batter swings and misses the ball completely on the third strike *and* the pitch is not caught (in the air) by the catcher *and* first base was unoccupied at the time, then the batter can attempt to advance. To get him out, the catcher can throw the ball to the first baseman who must tag first base before the runner arrives or a fielder can just tag the batter out before he reaches first base. Usually, the catcher is able to just pick up the ball and tag the batter. I knew that I would get letters if I didn't include this rule.

# How Did You Do?

In the test chapters, there were nine questions with one point credit for a correct answer. On five of these questions, you could also lose one point for a wrong answer.

If you finished with a positive score, you know baseball. Even if you just understand the explanations, you understand baseball and will effortlessly add to your knowledge as you watch more games.

| Score | Hit category |
|-------|-------------|
| 9 | Grand slam! (A home run with the bases loaded) |
| 8 | Home run! |
| 7,6,5 | Double |
| 4,3 | Single |
| 2,1 | Walk |
| 0 | Pop out |
| -1 to -5 | Strike-out. Need to read the book again. |

What did you score? Send your score and questions, comments, or complaints to me with a stamped, self-addressed envelope.

John W. Hood, c/o Forward Publishing, P. O. Box 693, Tinley Park, IL 60477.

Every letter will be answered.

# Glossary/Index

**Note:** *These are general definitions. They are not intended to cover every aspect of the defined rule, baseball skill, etc. The number after each term indicates the page on which the term appears.*

**appeal.** 17. A fielder's special request for an umpire's ruling as to whether a runner illegally left his base and advanced to the next base before a fly ball was caught. See **leave early**

**at bat.** 68. A player's turn to swing at pitches. A batter who stands in the batter's box is 'at bat'. 'At bat' also refers to a completed turn in the batter's box. A player who took four turns batting during a game had four 'at bats'.

**back leg.** 28. The leg that a player pushes off of when batting or throwing. A batter pushes off the leg farther away from the pitcher to begin his swing; a right-handed fielder pushes off his right foot to throw.

**balk.** 82. A pitcher's motion which an umpire deems to have been made to intentionally deceive any base runner. Each runner on base is allowed to advance one base when a balk is called. When a pitcher attempts a pickoff throw, he must step directly toward the base (which the runner occupies). A pitcher is not permitted to make any of the motions normally associated with pitching to a batter, then throw to a base. The majority of balk calls are based on a violation of one of these two rules.

**ball.** 19, 21. A pitch that does not pass through the strike zone and that the batter does not swing at.

**base hit.** 44,45. A batting statistic. A 'hit' is a batted ball on which the batter's safe advance to first base or farther is not the result of 1) a fielder's error or 2) a fielder's choice. Generally speaking, whether a batter is credited with a single, double, triple, or home run is determined by the official scorer's judgment as to how far the batter would advance if the fielders played errorlessly and concentrated solely on getting the batter out or preventing his advance.

**base on balls.** 19, 21. The award of first base occupancy to the batter after four balls are called.

**base runner.** 9. An offensive player who occupies a base when a batter is at bat. However, a batter may also be referred to as a base runner when running after hitting a ball.

**bases loaded.** 13. First, second, and third base are occupied by base runners.

**bat.** 3. A wooden or aluminum club that is used to hit a baseball.

**bat, to.** 4. A player's act of standing in the batter's box with his bat awaiting the pitcher's pitch.

**batter**. 4. The player whose turn it is to bat.

**batting average.** 45, 68. A batting statistic which represents the percentage of at bats in which the batter got a base hit. It is figured by dividing total hits by 'official' at bats. A walk, hit-by-pitch, sacrifice fly, or successful sacrifice bunt are not counted as official at bats because the batter is deemed not to have had a fair opportunity to get a hit or to have intentionally given up his chance to get a hit.

**batting order.** 5. The nine players in the game bat in turn in accordance with this list.

**block a base.** 76. A fielder's act of physically obstructing a runner's access to a base. Professional players are permitted to block a base when they have possession of, or are in the act of catching, a ball.

**breaking ball.** 32. The curveball and slider. They are called breaking balls because they move or 'break' to the side.

**break up the attempted double play.** 76. A forced base runner's act of intentionally sliding into the fielder in order to disrupt his throw to first base.

**brushback pitch.** 38. A pitch intentionally thrown close to the batter. The purpose of a brushback pitch is to induce in the batter the fear of being hit by a pitch. The batter's reactions to the next pitch will generally be more mechanical and less instinctive.

**bunt.** 52. A batter's technique of holding the bat horizontally and letting the ball hit it, instead of swinging. A good bunt will roll about half the way to first or third base.

**call.** 21. An umpire's judgment. An umpire is responsible for calling a pitch a 'ball' or a 'strike', calling a batted ball 'fair' or 'foul', calling a runner 'safe' or 'out', as well as enforcing other rules.

**can of corn.** 24. Slang for a high fly ball that is easy to catch.

**change speeds.** 37. A pitcher's practice of throwing different types of pitches to a batter. Each different type of pitch (fastball, curveball, slider, change-up) travels at a different speed. Using the different pitches, or changing speeds, prevents the batter from being able to anticipate a particular pitch and time his swing accordingly.

**change-up.** 32. A slow pitch or slowball.

**cleanup hitter.** 49. The batter in the fourth spot in the batting order. Traditionally, he is a power hitter who attempts to drive in base runners, or 'clean up' the bases with a long hit.

**close pitch.** 62. A pitch near the strike zone and which may be called a 'ball' or a 'strike' by the umpire.

**closer.** 66. The relief pitcher who is brought in to finish pitching the game. He is usually a good strike-out pitcher who enters the game in the ninth inning when his team is ahead.

**complete game.** 65. A pitching statistic stating that a starting pitcher pitched every inning of a game.

**concede the run.** 78. When, on a batted ball, the fielding team does not attempt to get a runner out at home plate. Instead, a fielder throws the ball to another base to prevent the batter and/or another runner from advancing farther.

**contact hitter.** 52. A batter who infrequently swings and misses.

**control.** 34, 37. The ability of a pitcher to throw different types of pitches in desired locations.

**count.** 35. The total of balls and strikes on a batter at a given moment. Balls are stated first, so a count of 1-2 means that there is one ball and two strikes on the batter.

**cover, to.** 51. A fielder's act of standing on, or over, a base awaiting a potential throw.

**curveball.** 32. A pitch that moves to the side and down just before reaching home plate. A right-handed pitcher's curveball will move to his left and down.

**cut off man.** 79. An infielder who stands in line with, and well in front of, the base to which an outfielder is throwing. If the runner attempting to advance to that base will clearly be safe, then the infielder catches, or cuts off, the throw. Cutting off the throw effectively prevents other runners from advancing.

**cut off throw.** 79. An outfielder's throw to a cut off man.

**deep.** 46. The outfield depth nearest the fence or wall.

**designated hitter.** 50. A position player who bats in the place of the pitcher in American League games. (In Major League Baseball, there are two Leagues, the American and the National.) At some amateur levels of baseball, a designated hitter is allowed to bat for any player.

**double.** 44. A hit on which the batter is able to advance to second base.

**double play.** 12. A play on which the defensive team gets two outs during continuous action. The three most common types of double play are as follows: (1) A ground ball on which a runner is forced out at a base and the fielder who makes the force out relays the ball to first base to get the batter out, (2) A caught line drive or fly ball in which the fielder (in possession of the ball) also gets the runner out by tagging the base before the runner can tag up, (3) A pitch on which the batter strikes-out and the runner, who is attempting to steal, is thrown out.

**down the line.** 46. An expression used to describe a ball that is hit close to one of the foul lines.

**drive the runner(s) in.** 49. A batted ball which enables a runner, or runners, to score.

**earned run.** 70. A pitching statistic stating runs which scored, minus runs which scored as a result of a fielder's error. Earned runs are charged to the pitcher who put the scoring runner on base to determine earned run average or ERA.

**earned run average.** 70. A pitching statistic indicating the average number of earned runs yielded by a pitcher per nine innings.

**ERA.** See **earned run average**

**error.** 44. A fielding statistic. An error is a fielder's misplay, such as dropped fly ball, bobbled ground ball, or dropped throw. As a result of the misplay, a batter who would be otherwise out is safe or a runner advances.

**extra base hit.** 69. A double, triple, or home run.

**extra innings.** 96. Additional innings played in order to break a tie score after the regulation number of innings have been played. For baseball games through the high school level, seven innings constitutes a regulation game. For higher levels, nine innings is a regulation game.

**fair.** 7. A ground ball that is first touched, or stops, before reaching first or third base when on or between the first and third base foul lines; for ground balls passing first or third base without being touched, the ball is fair if it passed over, or to the infield side of, first or third base; a fly ball touched or landing in fair territory beyond first or third base.

**fair territory.** 7. That portion of the field between and including the foul lines.

**fastball.** 31. The type of pitch that is thrown with the greatest speed.

**field a ball.** 11. To catch a batted or thrown ball.

**field cleanly.** 40. To catch a thrown or batted ball without bobbling or muffing it.

**fielder.** 4. A defensive player. Each defensive fielder has a position.

**fielder's choice.** 44. Generally, a play on which a fielder obviously could have gotten the batter out but tries to get an out on a runner instead.

**fly ball.** 6. Any ball that is hit in the air.

**force.** 10. A batted ball on which a runner must attempt to advance one base safely. When a batter hits a fair batted fall that hits the ground

— and there is a runner occupying first base or runners occupying first and second base or runners occupying first, second, and third base — then each such runner must attempt to advance one base.

**force at every base.** 13. A situation in which the bases are loaded. There is a potential force out at second base, third base, and home plate if the batter hits a fair ground ball. The fielders could, of course, also attempt to get an out at first base (on the batter).

**force is off.** 18. When the fielder gets an out on batter A or runner A who would force runner B then a force is no longer in effect on runner B.

**force out.** 12. When a force is in effect, the fielder in possession of the ball gets an out by tagging the base (to which a runner was forced to attempt to advance) before the runner tags the base.

**force play.** See **force out**

**foul.** 7. A fly ball that lands in foul territory beyond first or third base or is touched while in the air anywhere over foul territory; ground ball that stops, or is first touched, before reaching first or third base when outside the first or third base line; an untouched ground ball that passes outside of first or third base.

**foul ball.** See **foul**

**foul line.** 7. White chalk lines that divide the field into fair and foul territory. The line itself is part of fair territory.

**foul off.** 56. The act of hitting a ball foul.

**foul territory.** 7. The area outside the foul lines.

**fundamentally sound.** 65. The ability of a player or a team to execute routine plays.

**gap.** 47. The area between the center fielder and the left fielder or the center fielder and the right fielder.

**get on base.** 49. To advance to a base by hit or walk.

**get the ball down.** 81. The act of bunting a pitch on the ground in fair territory. For example, on a suicide squeeze, the batter's job is to 'get the ball down'.

**glove.** 4. A leather covering for the hand worn by fielders on their non-throwing hand. A glove has a separate section for each finger. The glove is hinged and connected by a leather webbing between the thumb and index finger sections.

**goes through.** 63. A batted ball which gets past the infielders and goes into the outfield. Usually refers to a line drive. A runner on third base exercises good judgment when he does not start running until a line drive 'goes through' (the infield).

**going halfway.** 77. A runner's technique of running partway to the next base while he waits to see if a fly ball will be caught. If the ball is not caught, the runner will have a head start to the next base. If the ball is caught, the runner will retreat to tag the base that he occupied when the ball was hit.

**going on the pitch.** 77. A runner's act of starting to run to the next base just as the pitcher begins to throw a pitch. When a runner attempts to steal a base, he 'goes on the pitch'.

**good jump.** 77. A term describing a runner who gets a good running start off the base hit he occupies. If a runner leaves a base too early, he may be picked off. A runner who starts for the next base at the split second that the pitcher begins his pitching motion is said to get a 'good jump'.

**good move.** 82. The ability of a pitcher, when a runner is on first base, to make an effective pickoff throw to first base. A throw can be effective because the pitcher uses a quick move or is able to disguise whether he is going to throw a pitch (or throw to first base) until the last moment.

**good strike.** 33. A particular type of pitch thrown in a desired location in the strike zone. For example, a change-up or curveball is usually thrown in the low and outside part of the strike zone. A very good fastball or slider may be thrown anywhere in the strike zone except 'down the middle' of the plate.

**ground ball.** 6. A batted ball that bounces along the ground.

**grounder.** See **ground ball**

**hit.** See **base hit**

**hit-and-run.** 52. An offensive play used with a runner on first base. The runner 'goes on the pitch'. The batter then tries to hit the ball through the area vacated by the fielder (the second baseman or shortstop) who covers second base.

**hitter's pitch.** The next pitch when the batter has a 3-1 count. On a 3-1 count the pitcher often throws a fastball which is the easiest pitch to hit. The batter will swing at a strike instead of taking the pitch because he does not want to have two strikes against him.

**hit the outside corner.** 29, 36. A pitch that passes through the part of the strike zone farthest away from the batter. The term generally refers to a low and outside pitch.

**hit the ball where it is pitched.** To hit outside pitches to the opposite field and pull other pitches.

**hitting behind the runner.** 86. A right-handed batter's technique of intentionally hitting the ball to the 'opposite field' with no outs. The batter hits to right field to enable a runner on second base to advance to third base. The runner will usually be able to advance even if the batter makes an out on a ground ball or fly ball.

**hold a runner close.** 82. A pitcher's ability to minimize the size of the runner's lead by using 'pickoff throws' to upset the runner's timing.

**holding a runner on base.** 57. The positioning of the first baseman next to first base in order to receive pickoff throws from the pitcher.

**hole, the.** 47. The space about midway between the shortstop and the third baseman, as in, 'The shortstop fielded a ground ball in the hole.'

**home plate umpire.** 21. The official who stands behind home plate. His major responsibility is to call each pitch a ball or strike.

**home run.** 44. A hit in which the batter circles the bases to score a run. When a batter hits a ball over the outfield fence in fair territory, he is automatically credited with a home run and ceremoniously trots around the bases.

**hot corner.** 42. The third baseman's position. The third baseman must field many hard-hit balls because he is positioned relatively close to the batter and there are more right-handed batters (who pull the ball to the left side of the infield) than left-handed batters.

**indicator.** 58. A signal given by the third base coach which immediately precedes the signal for an offensive play (such as the steal, hit-and-run, or sacrifice bunt).

**infield fly rule.** 24. A rule stating that when, with less than two outs, a batter hits a catchable fly ball in the infield with runners on first and second base, or with the bases loaded, the batter is automatically out.

**inning.** 5. A unit of play in a baseball game which is completed after each team has made three outs.

**inside-the-park home run.** 44. A hit that does not leave the ballpark in which the batter circles the bases to score.

**intentional walk.** 83. A pitcher's act of throwing four 'balls' to the batter on purpose. The pitches are thrown a couple of feet outside home plate.

**lead off batter.** 49. The first batter to bat in an inning. The lead off batter in the batting order is the batter who is scheduled to bat first.

**lead runner.** 63. The runner on base who has made the most progress around the bases. If there are runners on first and second base, the runner on second base is the lead runner.

**leave early.** 17. A runner who tags his base and attempts to advance (illegally) on a fly ball before the ball is touched by a fielder.

**left-center.** 46. The area of the field midway between left field and center field.

**line drive.** 6. A hard-hit ball with a flat or very slight arc.

**long reliever.** 66. A pitcher who replaces another pitcher (usually the starting pitcher) in the early or middle innings of a game.

**loss.** 71. A team loses a game when the other team scores more runs than it does. A 'loss' is also a pitching statistic. A pitcher is charged with a loss when a batter to whom he pitched scores run that gives the other team its last lead (in a game that the pitcher's team loses).

**mental mistakes.** 65. A player's exercise of poor judgment. Examples of mental mistakes include throwing an 0-2 pitch 'down the middle', a runner failing to run on a batted ball when there are two outs, a batter swinging at a pitch that would be called a 'ball' on a 3-0 count, and a fielder throwing to the wrong base.

**middle, the.** 47. The infield area around second base.

**middle reliever.** 66. See **long reliever**

**mitt.** 4. A type of glove used by the catcher. The thumb fits in one section and the other fingers all fit in the other section. The mitt is heavily padded.

**mound.** The raised dirt hill in the middle of the infield on which the pitcher stands.

**movement.** 31. The change of direction on a pitch. A pitcher has good movement on his fastball when it breaks to the side and down.

**official scorer.** 46. An objective observer who decides whether a particular play should be a hit or an error and determines whether, on a hit, a batter will be credited with a single, double, triple, or home run.

**on deck circle.** 50. An area near the dugout, defined by a chalk circle, where the next better awaits his turn to bat.

**opposite field.** 28. The side of the field opposite to the side to which a batter naturally pulls the ball. A right-handed batter pulls the ball to left field so right field is the 'opposite field' for a right-handed batter.

**out.** 5. The defensive team's objective in a baseball game; preventing a runner or batter from occupying a base.

**out on strikes.** 22. See **strike-out**

**overmanaging.** 87. Overuse of offensive strategy.

**pickoff throw.** 57. A pitcher's throw to a fielder covering a base in an attempt to get the runner out or 'hold the runner close'.

**pinch hitter.** 66. A substitute who bats for, and takes the place of, a player in the batting order.

**pitch.** 3. A throw by the pitcher to the catcher that the batter may try to hit.

**pitchout.** 83. A fast pitch intentionally thrown about a foot outside the outside edge of home plate. The pitchout is used to defend against the steal or hit-and-run play.

**pivot.** 41. A fielder's act of repositioning his feet in order to make a throw after fielding a ball or catching a throw.

**play is on.** 59. A term meaning that an offensive strategy such as a steal, sacrifice bunt, or hit-and-run is in effect.

**playing by the book.** 87. A manager's judicious use of strategy. Use of strategy only when the odds favor success or when necessary.

**playing in at the corners.** 80. A defensive strategy in which the first and third basemen take positions on the infield grass (and charge in a few more steps when the pitch is released). Used to defend against the sacrifice bunt.

**playing in on the grass.** 80. A defensive strategy in which all the infielders take positions on the infield grass. Used by the fielders in order to have a better chance to throw out a runner at home plate on a ground ball.

**playing the batter to pull.** 47. The positioning of the fielders when they expect a batter to pull the ball. Instead of playing straightaway, each fielder takes a position a few steps to the left of a right-handed batter or a few steps to the right of a left-handed batter.

**playing the infield in.** See **playing in on the grass**

**pop fly.** See **pop-up**

**pop-up.** 6. A fly ball in the infield area.

**position.** The place on the field where a defensive player stands. Names of the positions are pitcher, catcher, first baseman, second baseman, shortstop, third baseman, left fielder, central fielder, and right fielder.

**position player.** 48. A player who plays a position other than pitcher.

**power.** 29. To hit a pitch hard and far.

**power hitter.** 45. A player who hits many home runs and doubles.

**protecting the runner.** 56. A batter's act of making contact with a pitch on a hit-and-run play (including fouling off a pitch) so the runner will not be at risk of being thrown out at second base.

**pulling the ball.** 28. A right-handed batter's act of hitting to the left side of the field (between second base or center field and the left field line) and a left-handed batter's act of hitting to the right side of the field (between second base or center field and the right field foul line). A batter naturally hits the ball harder when he pulls the ball.

**range.** 72, 80. The amount of ground that a fielder covers on batted balls. A fielder has good range if he covers a lot of ground.

**RBI.** See **run batted in**

**relay man.** 78. The infielder who, when a throw to a base is too far for an outfielder to make, intercepts the outfielder's throw and throws it to the base.

**relief pitcher.** 65. A pitcher who replaces another pitcher during the game.

**right-center.** 47. The area of the field about midway between right field and center field.

**run.** 8. The only scoring unit in baseball. A run is scored when a runner crosses home plate before three outs are made unless the third out is made on a Must Play. Also a runner must cross home plate before another runner is tagged out for the third out.

**run batted in.** 69. A batting statistic. A batter is credited with one run batted in or RBI when a runner scores as a result of a batter's batted ball or the batter's walking or being hit by a pitch with the bases loaded. A batter is not credited with an RBI if a run scores as a result of the batter hitting into a double play.

**runner.** See **base runner**

**run the ball in.** 64. The practice of an infielder or outfielder in the shallow part of the outfield running into the infield with the ball to prevent a runner from advancing. The fielder runs the ball in to keep from having to make a throw when the runner will not advance anyway.

**sacrifice bunt.** 51, 52. An offensive strategy in which the batter bunts in order to enable a runner to advance. The batter, who is out at first base while the runner or runners advance, is deemed to have intentionally made an out or sacrificed his chance to get a hit.

**sacrifice fly.** 17. A fly ball caught for an out on which a runner is able to tag up and score.

**safe.** 11. The advance of a base runner or a batter to a base, or a runner's return to a base, without making an out. The batter or runner is allowed to occupy such base.

**safety squeeze.** 81. An offensive strategy in which the batter bunts and the runner on third base decides whether to try to score.

**scoring position.** 51. A runner on second base. A runner on second base will ordinarily be able to score on any hit in which the ball goes into the outfield.

**set position.** 57. The stance that a pitcher assumes with a runner, or runners, on base. The pitcher does not wind up, but stands sideways with his back foot on the pitching rubber (a right-handed pitcher faces third base). Before pitching or attempting a pickoff throw, the pitcher must come to a momentary stop while holding the ball in front of him. The set position is used by pitchers at levels above Little League.

**shaking off the sign.** 33. A shake of the head or glove by the pitcher to indicate that he is rejecting the pitch that the catcher signalled.

**shallow.** 46. The outfield depth closest to the infield.

**short reliever.** 66. A pitcher who replaces another pitcher during the last few innings of the game or late innings.

**signals.** 53. See **signs**

**signs.** 58. Secret, coded communications which are transmitted from coaches to players on the same team. The third base coach signals offensive plays to the batter and runner(s) and the catcher signals a pitch to the pitcher.

**single.** 44. A hit on which the batter is able to advance as far as first base.

**slide.** 75. A runner's technique of skidding along the ground on his hip or stomach in order to stop on a base or to avoid a fielder's tag.

**slider.** 31. A type of pitch. A slider is thrown almost as fast as a fastball and also curves and drops, but less dramatically than the curveball.

**square around to bunt.** 51, 89. A term for a type of batting stance in which the batter turns his body to face the pitcher holding the bat horizontally over home plate. The batter squares around to attempt a sacrifice bunt.

**squeeze.** See **squeeze play**

**squeeze play.** 81. An offensive strategy in which the batter bunts in an attempt to drive in a runner from third base. (see also **safety squeeze** and **suicide squeeze**)

**starting pitcher.** 65. The pitcher who begins the game for a team.

**steal.** 51. A runner's successful advance of one base during a pitch (on which there is no batted ball).

**steal the signs.** 58. To decipher the other team's signs.

**straightaway.** 47. The defensive positioning when playing the batter not to pull. The center fielder will be in line with home plate and second base. The left and right fielders will be the same distance from center fielder and the left and right field foul lines, respectively. The first and third basemen will each be the same distance from their respective foul lines as will the shortstop and second baseman.

**stretch.** 57. See **set position**

**strike.** 20. A pitch that passes through the strike zone which the batter takes, a pitch at which the batter swings and misses, or pitch that the batter hits foul that is not caught in the air.

**strike-out.** 20. An automatic out made when three strikes are charged to a batter during a time at bat, except that the batter does not strike-out if the third strike is a foul ball that hits the ground. But he does strike-out if he bunts a ball foul on the third strike.

**strike zone.** 20. The area over home plate between the top of the batter's knees and the bottom of his breastbone as determined when he assumes his batting stance.

**suicide squeeze.** 81. An offensive play in which the runner on third base goes on the pitch and the batter bunts.

**sweet spot.** 29. The area of the bat between two-thirds and three-quarters of the distance from the bottom of the bat to the top. The ball springs off of the bat when hit there.

**swing.** 28. The batter's act of moving the bat in an arc in an attempt to hit a pitched ball.

**swing late.** 28. To trigger the swing too late either to 'pull' or to make contact with a pitch.

**switch-hitter.** 27. A batter who can bat either right or left-handed.

**tag.** 11. A fielder's touching of a runner with the ball or touching a base, or a runner's touching of a base.

**tagging up.** 15. A runner's act of touching the base that he occupies after a fly ball is caught.

**take, to.** 35. To not swing at a pitch.

**take a lead.** 56. A runner's act of standing several feet away from a base as the pitcher stands on the mound.

**throw behind the runner.** 64. Throwing to a base to which the runner has already advanced instead of the base to which the runner is heading.

**time.** 15. A stoppage of play called by an umpire.

**time-out.** See **time**

**triple.** 44. A hit on which the batter is able to advance to third base.

**umpire.** 8, 21. An official who calls 'balls' and 'strikes', calls batted balls 'fair' and 'foul', calls batters and runners 'safe' or 'out', and makes all rule interpretations.

**unearned run.** 70. A run which would not have scored, but for an error.

**utility man.** 43. A position player who can play more than one position.

**walk.** See **base on balls**

**win.** 71. A team wins a game when it scores more runs than the other team in a completed game. A 'win' is also a pitching statistic. A pitcher is credited with a win when he is in the game when his team takes its last lead.

**wind up.** 56. A pitching motion used to generate momentum. The pitcher rocks backward before stepping forward to release the pitch.

**won-lost record.** 71. A pitching statistic stating the number of games a pitcher is credited with winning followed by the number of losses that he is charged with.

# Acknowledgements

## Announcing my All-Star team!

The support and plain old hard work of team members made this book possible and better. Their cooperation and quick turn-around time on their work are enormously appreciated.

My parents, Dorothy and Charles Hood, are my Most Valuable Players. They offered continuing encouragement and the dollars that kept me liquid.

My brother, Tom Hood, is a true ResBex. His thorough manuscript reviews were extremely helpful.

Susan Alcazar, my friend, proofed and criticized early drafts and offered continuing support of this project.

Dave Allen, free lance artist, produced the great cover.

Ron Anderson and Frank Ganser, the head baseball coaches for the two Tinley Park High Schools, reviewed early drafts for technical accuracy.

Wendy Luna, Partners in Design, formatted the text beautifully. Thanks also to her capable assistant, Bill Quilhot, her father.

Rich McCoy, free lance artist, did the outstanding text illustrations.

Len Overcash, professional technical writer and free lance writer, was my main proofreader for grammar and punctuation. Len straightened out many crooked sentences.

Marge Prince, free lance writer, proofed drafts. Nothing got past her.

Martin Zabell, a friend, is a former baseball writer who now operates Z Write Stuff, which advises businesses on the use of the print medium. Martin gave valuable help in a couple of areas.

Rich Zubaty, author of the popular book *Surviving the Feminization of America,* is my frequent breakfast buddy. Rich's insights were simply invaluable.

Others, all published writers, who offered great critiques and did unglamorous proofreading chores were Janet Holan, Eleanor McKay, Ardis Stewart, and Helen Tessmer.

Thanks also to the best baseball color commentators in the business, Steve Stone and Lou Boudreau, for their encouragement.

Thanks to my team. Any errors are mine.

# ORDER FORM

**Why They Scratch Themselves** makes a great gift!

To order a copy of **Why They Scratch Themselves** return this form with a check or money order for $13.45.  ($9.95 plus $3.50 shipping and handling) payable to:

➡ **Forward Press, P.O. Box 693, Tinley Park, IL 60477**

Name _____

Address _____

City_____ State_____ Zip _____

❏ Send me a copy of **Why They Scratch Themselves.**

OR

# CALL TOLL FREE
# 1-800-35 BOOKS
### (1-800-352-6657)

Use **Why They Scratch Themselves** as a fund-raiser for your organization! Send for our free brochure telling you how to do it!

✓ Just fill out your name and address on the order form,
✓ enclose a stamped, self-addressed envelope and
✓ check this box:

❏ Please send me the free fund-raising brochure.

John Hood ('51) is a lawyer concentrating in employment law.

Hood has been infatuated with baseball since he was old enough to hold a bat. He has explained the game so many times in so many ways both to his friends and in seminars, that he was inspired to write this simple, easy-to-read book.

A Chicagoan, Hood claims to have been a Chicago Cub fan since he was conscious.